MW00772029

Puzzles in Logic, Languages
and Computation

Recreational Linguistics

Volume 1

For further volumes:
http://www.springer.com/series/11630

Dragomir Radev

Editor

Puzzles in Logic, Languages and Computation

The Red Book

 Springer

Editor
Dragomir Radev
Department of Electrical Engineering and Computer Science
School of Information, Department of Linguistics
University of Michigan
Ann Arbor, MI, USA

Foreword by
James Pustejovsky
Brandeis University
Department of Computer Science
Volen Center for Complex Systems
Waltham, MA, USA

ISBN 978-3-642-34377-3   ISBN 978-3-642-34378-0 (eBook)
DOI 10.1007/978-3-642-34378-0
Springer Heidelberg New York Dordrecht London

Library of Congress Control Number: 2013931838

© Springer-Verlag Berlin Heidelberg 2013
This work is subject to copyright. All rights are reserved by the Publisher, whether the whole or part of the material is concerned, specifically the rights of translation, reprinting, reuse of illustrations, recitation, broadcasting, reproduction on microfilms or in any other physical way, and transmission or information storage and retrieval, electronic adaptation, computer software, or by similar or dissimilar methodology now known or hereafter developed. Exempted from this legal reservation are brief excerpts in connection with reviews or scholarly analysis or material supplied specifically for the purpose of being entered and executed on a computer system, for exclusive use by the purchaser of the work. Duplication of this publication or parts thereof is permitted only under the provisions of the Copyright Law of the Publisher's location, in its current version, and permission for use must always be obtained from Springer. Permissions for use may be obtained through RightsLink at the Copyright Clearance Center. Violations are liable to prosecution under the respective Copyright Law.
The use of general descriptive names, registered names, trademarks, service marks, etc. in this publication does not imply, even in the absence of a specific statement, that such names are exempt from the relevant protective laws and regulations and therefore free for general use.
While the advice and information in this book are believed to be true and accurate at the date of publication, neither the authors nor the editors nor the publisher can accept any legal responsibility for any errors or omissions that may be made. The publisher makes no warranty, express or implied, with respect to the material contained herein.

Printed on acid-free paper

Springer is part of Springer Science+Business Media (www.springer.com)

To Axinia, Laura, and Victoria

Foreword

By
James Pustejovsky
TJX/Feldberg Professor of Computer Science
Brandeis University

This book brings together, for the first time in one collection, the best English-language problems created for students competing in the Computational Linguistics Olympiad. These problems are representative of the diverse areas presented in the competition and designed with three principles in mind:

- To challenge the student analytically, without requiring any explicit knowledge or experience in linguistics or computer science;

- To expose the student to the different kinds of reasoning required when encountering a new phenomenon in a language, both as a theoretical topic and as an applied problem.

- To foster the natural curiosity students have about the workings of their own language, as well as to introduce them to the beauty and structure of other languages.

The Linguistics Olympiad is designed to develop metalinguistic reasoning that is useful for any career involving human language and also to foster analytical problem-solving skills that are relevant for many technical and non-technical careers. The problems represented in this volume also emphasize an aptitude for computational thinking more than linguistics Olympiads in other countries. In addition to using logical and analytical skills, they explicitly focus on concepts and tools from computer science, such as finite state machines and graph search, while also introducing applications of computational linguistics, such as machine translation, information extraction, and automatic summarization.

Aside from being a fun intellectual challenge, the Olympiad mimics the skills used by researchers and scholars in the field of computational linguistics, which is increasingly important for the United States and other countries. Using computational linguistics, these experts can develop automated technologies such as translation software that cut down on the time and training needed to work with other languages, or software that automatically produces informative English summaries of documents in other languages or answers questions about information in these documents. In an increasingly global economy where businesses operate across borders and languages, having a strong pool of computational linguists is a competitive advantage, and an important component to both security and growth in the 21st century.

This collection of problems for the linguistics Olympiad is not only a valuable resource for high school students wishing to prepare themselves for the competition, but is a wonderful general introduction to the field of linguistics through the analytic problem solving technique.

Preface to Volume I

This two-volume set includes more than 100 original problems (and their solutions) in (traditional) linguistics and computational linguistics. Many of the problems were used in the first five installments of NACLO[1] (North American Computational Linguistics Olympiad). NACLO, inaugurated in 2007, is an annual competition for high school students interested in human languages as well as the ways in which humans and computers deal with them using logic. NACLO is modeled after the IOL[2] (International Linguistics Olympiad) but, unlike IOL, includes a large percentage of problems in formal and computational linguistics. NACLO is a part of ELCLO (the consortium of English-language computational linguistics Olympiads, which includes Australia, Ireland, and Great Britain in addition to NACLO's members, USA and Canada).

This collection has been edited and augmented in order to make it appealing to a variety of audiences, from middle and high school students interested in languages, to teachers of languages, linguistics, and computer science, and to anyone fascinated by the phenomena of human language. All problems include detailed solutions that indicate how one can reach the answer even without any knowledge about the specific language or phenomenon on which the problems are based. The authors of the problems are linguistics and computer science professors and students and include several past contestants in the IOL, NACLO, and similar competitions.

The history of linguistics Olympiads started in 1965 in Russia when Andrey Zaliznyak organized the first local competition. Other contests followed in Eastern Europe. The first such contest in the USA was run in 1998-2000 by Thomas Payne for students in the Eugene, Oregon area. A hiatus followed and it was not until 2007 that another competition took place in North America. This time it was run nationwide in the USA and Canada. A number of students were able to participate remotely by having their high school teachers monitor the competition locally and send their papers to the NACLO committee for grading. The founders of NACLO include Tanya Korelsky (NSF) and also Lori Levin (CMU) and Thomas Payne (U. Oregon), as NACLO co-chairs, James Pustejovsky (Brandeis), as sponsorship chair, and Dragomir Radev (U. Michigan), as program chair and head coach of the US teams. A smaller and easier contest has also been held since 2007 by Aleka Blackwell in the Murphreesboro, TN area.

At the international level, a competition has taken place since 2003. It has been held ten times so far and has been hosted by Russia, Estonia, Poland, Bulgaria, the Netherlands, the USA, Slovenia, and Sweden. The eleventh IOL is scheduled for Manchester, UK in 2013. The international linguistics Olympiads have been modeled after similar competitions in Mathematics, Physics, Informatics, Biology, Chemistry, and other subjects. As of 2012, the strongest teams in Linguistics at the international level are the United States, Russia, Bulgaria, and Poland as well as the Netherlands, the United Kingdom, South Korea, and Latvia.

---

[1] http://www.naclo.cs.cmu.edu
[2] http://www.ioling.org

The goal of NACLO from its inception has been to popularize language and language technologies to high school students and to encourage them to pursue careers in these fields of study. Approximately 40% of all contestants in NACLO so far have been female. The very first NACLO winner was also female. The list of all NACLO winners so far includes: Rachel Zax (Ithaca, NY – 2007), Guy Tabachnick (New York, NY – 2008), Anand Natarajan (San Jose, CA – 2009), Ben Sklaroff (Palo Alto, CA – 2010), Daniel Mitropolsky (Oakville, Ontario, Canada – 2011), and Alex Wade (Reno, NV – 2012).

NACLO contestants can participate in two ways – at a university site nearby (if one exists) or at their own high school. The format is the same in both cases. The first round involves around 5-7 problems in a three hour time slot whereas the second (invitational) round includes 6-10 problems and takes 5 hours. Since 2010, first round problems have been graded by an auto-grading program while the second round problems are manually graded by the NACLO volunteer jury.

A large number of US students have performed extremely well at the ILO. The awards received form a really long list that includes over the past six years, the following: six out of 22 individual gold medals, four out of 7 team gold medals, and three out of five combined gold medals. The performance by year is shown here:

2007 Individual Gold (rank 1 of 3): Adam Hesterberg, Seattle, WA
    Team Gold (tied): Rebecca Jacobs, Joshua Falk, Michael Gottlieb, and Anna Tchetchetkine
2008 Individual Gold (rank 2 of 3): Hanzhi Zhu
    Team Gold (tied): Morris Alper, Rebecca Jacobs, Jae-kyu Lee, and Hanzhi Zhu
    Combined Gold: Josh Falk, Jeffrey Lim, Anand Natarajan, Guy Tabachnick
2009 Team Gold: Rebecca Jacobs, Anand Natarajan, Alan Huang, and Morris Alper
2010 Individual Gold (rank 3 of 3): Ben Sklaroff, Palo Alto, CA
    Combined Gold: Martin Camacho, Tian-Yi Damien Jiang, Alexander Iriza, and Alan Chang
2011 Individual Gold (rank 1 of 4): Morris Alper, Palo Alto, CA
    Team Gold: Morris Alper, Aaron Klein, Wesley Jones, and Duligur Ibeling
    Combined Gold: Morris Alper, Aaron Klein, Wesley Jones, and Duligur Ibeling
2012 Individual Gold (ranked 2 of 8): Alexander Wade, Reno, NV
    Individual Gold (ranked 4 of 8): Aderson Wang, PA
    Team Gold: Alexander Wade, Aidan Kaplan, Aaron Klein, and Erik Andersen

Other NACLO students who received medals at the international level:

Silver: Anand Natarajan (2008), Morris Alper (2008), Rebecca Jacobs (2009), Allen Yuan (2010), Martin Camacho (2010), Tian-Yi Damien Jiang (2010), Wesley Jones (2011), Allen Yuan (2011), Alexander Wade (2011), Duligur Ibeling (2011), Darryl Wu (2012), Aaron Klein (2012), Allan Sadun (2012).
Bronze: Jeffrey Lim (2008), Guy Tabachnick (2008), Rebecca Jacobs (2008), Alan Huang (2009), John Berman (2009), Sergei Bernstein (2009), Alexander Iriza (2010), Alan Chang (2010), Aaron Klein (2011), Daniel Mitropolsky (2011), Erik Andersen (2012).

More than 6,000 students have participated in NACLO so far. Each year, the top 100 (or so) get invited to the second "invitational" round which is used to determine the composition of the US and Canadian teams.

This book set includes two general classes of problems. The computational problems focus on formal and computational aspects of language understanding and automated language processing. The traditional problems pay more attention to linguistic phenomena such as morphology, phonology, phonetics, syntax, semantics, and pragmatics.

The traditional problems are on more than 50 languages and writing systems:
European/Middle Eastern: Ancient Greek, Swedish, Norwegian, Irish, Linear B, Bulgarian, Spanish, Armenian, Turkish, Romanian, Italian, Catalan, German, Etruscan, Hebrew, Welsh, Old Church Slavonic, Arabic, Russian, French, Greek, Albanian, English
Asian: Hmong, Huishu, Hindi, Japanese, Hmong, Tangkhul, Malayalam, Tamil, Vietnamese, Indonesian, Korean
Pacific: Ilocano, Manam Pile, Rotokas, Dyirbal, Abma, Minangkabau, Tanna, Arrernte, Warlpiri, Central Cagayan Agta, Hawaiian, Wembawemba, Pitjantjatjara, Nen, Enga
African: Swahili, Tadaksahak, Amharic, Maasai, Bambara
North and South American: Apinaye, Aymara, Tzolk'in, Quechua, Guaraní, Plains Cree, Tohono O'odham, Ulwa, Nahuatl, Ndyuka, Anishinaabemowin, Sahaptin, Zoque,

The computational problems cover: document retrieval, sentence similarity, optical character recognition, garden path sentences, semantics of noun-noun compounds, stemming, finite state automata, spectrograms, writing systems for the blind, spelling correction, text summarization, polarity induction, deixis, shift-reduce parsing, context-free grammars, named entity classification, text compression, machine translation, expansion of abbreviations, logical entailment, presupposition, word sense disambiguation, text processing, word reordering, syntactic ambiguity, handwriting recognition, word frequencies, syntactic transformations, recursion, modeling second language learning errors, sentence boundary identification, computational morphology, cognates, text classification, and Zipf's law.

In addition to the authors of the problems, I would like to thanks specifically the folks below for all their hard work over the years to make NACLO happen: Emily Bender, Mary Jo Bensasi, Marcus Berger, John Berman, Reed Blaylock, Eric Breck, Justin Brown, Rich Caneba, Hyunzoo Chai, Angie Chang, Ivan Derzhanski, Jason Eisner, Adam Emerson, Dominique Estival, Barbara di Eugenio, Jefferson Ezra, Eugene Fink, Anatole Gershman, Blumie Gourarie, Mercedes Harvey, Amy Hemmeter, Adam Hesterberg, Dick Hudson, Boris Iomdin, Alexander Iriza, Rebecca Jacobs, Ridley Jones, Wesley Jones, Tanya Korelsky, Nate LaFave, Andrew Lamont, Terry Langendoen, Rachael Leduc, Lillian Lee, Will Lewis, Pat Littell, Wanchen Lu, Rachel McEnroe, Ruslan Mitkov, Graham Morehead, David Mortensen, JP Obley, Martha Palmer, Tom Payne, Carrie Pichan, Ben Piche, Victor Pudeyev, James Pustejovsky, Vahed Qazvinian, Laura Radev, Adrienne Reed, Rahel Ringger, Meredith Rogan, David Ross, Andrea Sexton, Catherine Sheard, Ben Sklaroff, Catherine Arnott Smith, Noah Smith, Samuel Smolkin, Harold Somers, Richard Sproat, Kurnikova Stacy, Laine Stranahan, Rebecca Sundae, Jennifer Sussex, Roula Svorou, Aditya Tayade, Sally Thomason, Amy Troyani, Susanne Vejdemo, Zilin Wang, and Julia Workman.

The following organizations provided funding and other support for NACLO: the National Science Foundation, the Linguistics Society of America, the North American Chapter of the Association for Computational Linguistics, as well as Google, Yahoo!, Cambridge University Press, as well as many known and unknown supporters. They all deserve their own ticker tape parade for their contributions to NACLO.

How to use this book

The first volume contains 56 problems and the second one includes an additional 50. Based on the performance of the students in NACLO, each of the problems in the book set has been assigned a difficulty score from Beginner (one star) to Expert (five stars). Any person who has made it to high school has a shot at most of these problems. In fact, even the five-star problems were solved successfully during NACLO by dozens of high school students working under severe time pressure.

Problems of a more computational nature are marked with a small computer icon next to their names. The icon doesn't imply that a computer is needed to solve these problems but rather that they are related to computational linguistics.

The NACLO web site links to dozens of additional problems as well as numerous presentations, tutorials, and other educational materials for students and teachers alike.

Final words

In January 2011, the Linguistics Society of America awarded NACLO its "Linguistics, Language, and the Public" award for increasing awareness of linguistics in the general public. This honor is a strong indication of the recognition of the role that NACLO plays.

Dragomir Radev, NACLO Program Chair and US team head coach

September 30, 2012

Ann Arbor and New York

Table of Contents

List of Problems (1/2)

List of Problems (2/2)

List of Contributors

Morris Alper, Massachusetts Institute of Technology
Emily Bender, University of Washington
John Berman, Massachusetts Institute of Technology
Aleka Blackwell, Middle Tennessee State University
John Blatz, Google
Bozhidar Bozhanov, Consultant
Eric Breck, Google
Willie Costello, University of Pittsburgh
Ivan Derzhanski, Bulgarian Academy of Sciences
Erin Donnelly, University of California, Berkeley
Mark Dras, Macquarie University
Jason Eisner, Johns Hopkins University
Nicholas Evans, Australian National University
Eugene Fink, Carnegie Mellon University
Jeremy Hammond, Max Planck Institute
John Henderson, University of Western Australia
Adam Hesterberg, Massachusetts Institute of Technology
Richard Hudson, University College London
Boris Iomdin, Russian Academy of Sciences
Luda Kedova, University of Melbourne
Tanya Khovanova, Massachusetts Institute of Technology
Mary Laughren, University of Queensland
Lori Levin, Carnegie Mellon University
Patrick Littell, University of British Columbia
Daniel Midgley, University of Western Australia
Diego Mollá Aliod, Macquarie University
David Mortensen, University of Pittsburgh
Anand Natarajan, Stanford University
Rachel Nordlinger, University of Melbourne
Doris Payne, University of Oregon
Thomas Payne, University of Oregon
Eric Pederson, University of Oregon
Dragomir Radev, University of Michigan
Laura Radev, Chapin School
Verna Rieschild, Macquarie University
Noel Rude, Confederated Tribes of the Umatilla Indian Reservation
Cindy Schneider, University of New England
Ronnie Sim, SIL International
Jane Simpson, Australian National University
Harold Somers, Dublin City University
Richard Sproat, Google
Ankit Srivastava, Dublin City University
Todor Tchervenkov, Lyon Schools
Roy Tromble, Google
Julia Workman, University of Montana

Volume I
Problems

D. Radev (ed.), *Puzzles in Logic, Languages and Computation: The Red Book*, Recreational Linguistics 1,
DOI 10.1007/978-3-642-34378-0_1, © Springer-Verlag Berlin Heidelberg 2013

(1) We Are All Molistic in a Way (1/1)*

Imagine that you have heard these sentences:

1. Jane is molistic and slatty.
2. Jennifer is cluvious and brastic.
3. Molly and Kyle are slatty but danty.
4. The teacher is danty and cloovy.
5. Mary is blitty but cloovy.
6. Jeremiah is not only sloshful but also weasy.
7. Even though frumsy, Jim is sloshful.
8. Strungy and struffy, Diane was a pleasure to watch.
9. Even though weasy, John is strungy.
10. Carla is blitty but struffy.
11. The salespeople were cluvious and not slatty.

1.1. Then which of the following would you be likely to hear next?

a. Meredith is blitty and brastic.
b. The singer was not only molistic but also cluvious.
c. May found a dog that was danty but sloshful.

1.2. What quality or qualities would you be looking for in a person?

a. blitty
b. weasy
c. sloshful
d. frumsy

1.3. Explain all your answers. (Hint: The sounds of the words are not relevant to their meanings)

© Dragomir Radev, 2011. North American Computational Linguistics Olympiad, 2007 Round 1. This problem has been reproduced with the permission of the author.

(2) Pooh's Encyclopedia (1/1)**

Once upon a time, a very long time ago, Winnie-the-Pooh and his friends bought an electronic encyclopedia, and tried to find answers to several important questions:

Winnie-the-Pooh:
Where should a bear stock his jars of honey?
How much honey should a bear store for the winter?

Eeyore:
Where should I look for my lost tail?
Which animals sleep during the winter?

Christopher Robin:
What is the shortest way from my place to the house of Winnie-the-Pooh?
Who wrote the books about Pooh Bear?

The encyclopedia's search engine identified a number of articles related to their questions; for example, it returned the following matches:

Winter food storage (for Winnie-the-Pooh)
Sleep patterns in mammals and other animals (for Eeyore)
Short stories and movies about Winnie-the-Pooh (for Christopher Robin)
Writers of children's books (for Christopher Robin)

On the other hand, the search engine missed several other relevant articles; in particular, it did *not* retrieve the following articles:

Planning of food supplies
Lost-and-found agencies
Finding shortest paths on a map
Biography of A.A. Milne, the author of Winnie-the-Pooh

2.1.   Your task is to determine who received each of the following matches; two of these matches were for Winnie-the-Pooh, two for Eeyore, and two for Christopher Robin. Explain why!

Books about care and feeding of bears
Effects of honey on the sleep quality of humans and animals
Lost tales of "Bulls vs. Bears" stock trading
Ways to look for lost things
Ways to store food in the house
Winter hibernation of bears and rodents

© Eugene Fink, 2011. North American Computational Linguistics Olympiad, 2007 Round 1. This problem has been reproduced with the permission of the author.

(3) A Donkey in Every House (1/1)**

Consider these phrases in Ancient Greek (in a Roman-based transcription) and their unordered English translations:

(A) ho tōn hyiōn dulos   (1) the donkey of the master
(B) hoi tōn dulōn cyrioi   (2) the brothers of the merchant
(C) hoi tu emporu adelphoi   (3) the merchants of the donkeys
(D) hoi tōn onōn emporoi   (4) the sons of the masters
(E) ho tu cyriu onos   (5) the slave of the sons
(F) ho tu oicu cyrios   (6) the masters of the slaves
(G) ho tōn adelphōn oicos   (7) the house of the brothers
(H) hoi tōn cyriōn hyioi   (8) the master of the house

3.1. Place the number of the correct English translation in the space following each Greek sentence. Explain your answers!

3.2. Translate into Ancient Greek:

- the houses of the merchants;
- the donkeys of the slave

Note: The letter ō stands for a long **o**.

© Todor Tchervenkov, 2011. North American Computational Linguistics Olympiad, 2007 Round 1. This problem has been reproduced with the permission of the author.

(4) Hmong (1/1)**

Hmong Daw (which belongs to the Hmong Mien language family, along with several other Hmong languages) is spoken by approximately 165 thousand people in south-eastern China, Laos, Thailand, Vietnam, and some other countries.

In the 1960s, Shong Lue Yang, a peasant from the Hmong Daw nation (also known as White Miao), invented an original writing system for his native language. This writing system is still in use, alongside a Roman-based alphabet created by Christian missionaries.

Here are several words and phrases in the Hmong Daw language, written in Shong Lue Yang's script and in the missionaries' alphabet, as well as their English translations:

1.	ㅓ ⅢК ꙮᲚ	**kev ntsuas no**	degree
2.	ꙮⵏᲚ	**hauv**	inside
3.	ꙮꓱ Ꙣꓱ ꙮᴧ	**raug raws cai**	legal
4.	Ꙣꓴ ꙮᲚᲚ	**hloov mus**	transfer
5.	ꙮE	**qhua**	guest
6.	ꙮꙢᲚ ꙮᲚ ꙮᲚ	**yog los nag**	it is raining
7.	ꓕ ꙢꙢ	**kwv yees**	guess
8.	Ꙣꓱ ꙮᴧ ꓴᲚᲚ	**ris ceg luv**	Bermuda shorts

In the missionaries' alphabet the letter **w** stands for a specific vowel. The letters **g**, **s** and **v** at the ends of the syllables aren't consonants; instead, they denote the so-called tones (specific ways of pronouncing the vowels).

4.1. Write in the missionaries' alphabet (and explain):

9.	ꙮᲚᲚ	bird
10.	ꓕᴧ	lobster
11.	ꙮᲚᲚ ᲚᲚ	speak
12.	ꙮE ꙮᲚᲚ ᴧ	dizzy

4.2. Write in Shong Lue Yang's script (and explain):

13.	**hluav**	ash
14.	**li cas**	how?
15.	**neeg ntse**	smart, wise
16.	**yawg**	grandfather

© Ivan Derzhanski, 2011. North American Computational Linguistics Olympiad, 2007 Round 1. This problem has been reproduced with the permission of the author.

(5) Better Sorry than Shunk (1/1)***

Here is an English sentence with a nonsense verb in it (*in italics*):

"After the monster had *shunk* its prey, it dragged it back into the cave."

5.1. Fill in the other forms of this verb in the following sentences:

"She used to _____ groundhogs."
"Now she _____ possums for a living."
"When she was in Eugene she _____ thirty-three possums in one day."
"Then she took us possum-_____ in the Cascades."

5.2. Are there any other possible solutions to this problem? Please give all solutions, sorted by how likely they are correct, and explain your answer.

© Jason Eisner and Roy Tromble, 2011. North American Computational Linguistics Olympiad, 2007 Round 1. This problem has been reproduced with the permission of the authors.

(6) The Lost Tram (1/1)***

Consider these three text fragments:

(1) The tram makes no stops; you sit clown and are served; there are no further intrusions, no late-corners, no one hurrying to get off. The businessmen leaf through their financial reports, the lady with the hatbox is alone with her novel and her sirloin. Diners reading: you never see that on a plane. When the coast approaches arid dinner is over, everyone retires to his compartment to he transferred to the boat in peace, horizontally.
(Sunrise With Seamonsters, by Paul Theroux)

(2) Usually, Howie could legitimately claim to have no dear of any man or beast… Howie knew in his heart that it was he vulnerable positions he ended up in that scared him. He was used to operating from a position of strength, either real or projected. Now here he was, injured and alone, standing with and empty handgun in an open filed, while hid opponent or opponents fried their weapon from behind solid cover.
(Rough Justice, by Mark Johnstone)

(3) Two other factors effect the body's temperature regulation: age and acclimatization. As we grow older, we loose our ability to quickly regulate temperature… Very small children are also subject to heat disorders. There small size allows them to take on heat much faster then adults. They also cannot indicate their thirst, accept through irritability. They are completely dependent upon adults to make certain they get enough fluids.
(Doctor in the House: Your Best Guide to Effective Medical Self-Care, by John Harbert)

6.1. Each text contains some deviations from what the original author wrote. Try to find all the deviations and restore the original text.

6.2. For each text, explain why the deviations occurred.

6.3. Could you use a computer program to fix deviations of these types? If yes, how should it work?

© Boris Iomdin, 2011. North American Computational Linguistics Olympiad, 2007 Round 1. This problem has been reproduced with the permission of the author.

(7) Rewrite me Badd (1/1)*

You speak a little differently than your parents do. They probably say that you're speaking "bad English". Every generation of parents says this, but this is just how language works. In fact, this is where languages come from: enough generations of young people speaking "bad Latin", and eventually you have Spanish, French, and Italian!

Huishu is a language in the Tangkhulic family that is spoken in the easternmost part of India. Over time, enough changes occurred in this one village that the villagers now speak a different language than any of their neighboring villages. So, where they used to say "-lo" ("buy"), they now say "-lu", and where they used to say "-muk" ("cattle"), they now say "-mu?". (That symbol at the end represents the sound in the middle of "Uh-oh!", and the dashes in front just mean that these have to occur as parts of larger words.)

Linguists model historical sound changes as "string-rewrite rules". These are very much like a "find-and-replace" procedure in a word processor: look for one character or pattern, and replace it with another one. As the old language changed into modern Huishu, the following string-rewrite rules applied:

> **K-Insertion**: When you find an [u] at the end of the word, add a [k] after it.
> **Vowel-Raising**: When you find an [o] at the end of the word, replace it with [u].
> **K-Deletion**: When you find a [k] at the end of a word, replace it with [?].

These changes didn't all just happen at once, though. They happened one after another—although not necessarily in the order above!—and we can see in which order they happened by comparing the old forms to the new forms. Only one order will work; if these changes had happened in any other order, we would have different modern words.

7.1. Here are a few such pairs (the old form is at the top; the new one is at the bottom). From these, can you determine the order in which the above changes must have occurred? Write the names of the rules in the blanks on the left. The blanks in between each pair are for your benefit: if you write how each word changed as each rule applied, you should be able to work out their ordering in time.

Proto-Tangkhulic form:	-ru ("bone")	-khuk ("knee")	-ko ("nine")
Rule 1: _____			
Intermediate form 1: Rule 2: _____	_____	_____	_____
Intermediate form 2: Rule 3: _____	_____	_____	_____
Huishu form: _____	-ruk	-khu?	-ku

© Patrick Littell and David Mortensen, 2011. North American Computational Linguistics Olympiad, 2007 Round 1. This problem has been reproduced with the permission of the authors.

(8) This Problem is Pretty // Easy (1/1)***

True story: a major wireless company recently started an advertising campaign focusing on its claim that callers who use its phones experience fewer dropped calls.

The billboards for this company feature sentences that are split into two parts. The first one is what the recipient of the call hears, and the second one—what the caller actually said before realizing that the call got dropped. The punch line is that dropped calls can lead to serious misunderstandings. We will use the symbol // to separate the two parts of such sentences.

> (1) Don't bother coming // early.
> (2) Take the turkey out at five // to four.
> (3) I got canned // peaches.

These sentences are representative of a common phenomenon in language, called "garden path sentences". Psychologically, people interpret sentences incrementally, before waiting to hear the full text. When they hear the ambiguous start of a garden path sentence, they assume the most likely interpretation that is consistent with what they have heard so far. They then later backtrack in search of a new parse, should the first one fail.

In the specific examples above, on hearing the first part, one incorrectly assumes that the sentence is over. However, when more words arrive, the original interpretation will need to be abandoned.

> (4) All Americans need to buy a house // is a large amount of money.
> (5) Melanie is pretty // busy.
> (6) Fat people eat // accumulates in their bodies.

8.1. Come up with two examples of garden path sentences that are not just modifications of the ones above and of each other. Split each of these two sentences into two parts, and indicate how hearing the second part causes the hearer to revise his or her current parse.

For full credit, your sentences need to be such that the interpretation of the first part should change as much as possible on hearing the second part. For example, in sentence (6) above, the interpretation of the word "fat" changes from an adjective ("fat people") to a noun ("fat [that] people eat...").

Note: Sentences like "You did a great job..., // NOT!" don't count.

8.2. Rank sentences (4), (5), and (6), as well as the two sentences from your solution to 8.1. above, based on how surprised the hearer is after hearing the second part. What, in your opinion, makes a garden path sentence harder to process by the hearer?

© Dragomir Radev, 2011. North American Computational Linguistics Olympiad, 2007 Round 1. This problem has been reproduced with the permission of the author.

(9) Of Monkeys and Children (1/1)**

Apinayé belongs to the Ge language family of Brazil. Currently, it is spoken by less than 800 people, and therefore is seriously endangered. The following are some sentences in Apinayé, along with their English translations. You will see some letters here that do not occur in the English or Portuguese writing systems. You do not need to know exactly how these letters are pronounced in order to solve this problem:

Kukrɛ̃ kokoi.	'The monkey eats.'
Ape kra.	'The child works.'
Ape kokoi ratš.	'The big monkey works.'
Ape mï mɛtš.	'The good man works.'
Ape mɛtš kra.	'The child works well.'
Ape punui mï piŋetš.	'The old man works badly.'

9.1. Translate the following into English:

- Ape ratš mï mɛtš.
- Kukrɛ̃ ratš kokoi punui.
- Ape piŋetš mï.

9.2. Translate the following into Apinayé:

- 'The big child works a long time.'
- 'The old monkey eats a lot.'

9.3. Explain the meanings of the following words:

- ratš:
- mɛtš:
- piŋetš:

Previously published in: Payne, T. 2006. Exploring language structure: A student's guide. Cambridge, pp. 128.

© Ronnie Sim and Thomas Payne, 2011. North American Computational Linguistics Olympiad, 2008 Round 1. This problem has been reproduced with the permission of the authors.

(10) Springing up Baby (1/2)**

The following sentence pairs are translation equivalents in English and Hindi. There is not enough information in this data set to fully decode the Hindi from the English, but there is enough information to pinpoint the translations of certain words.

In particular, we are interested in the words **spring** and कल , each of which is ambiguous and translates differently in different cases.

The flowers bloom in the spring.
कलियाँ वसन्त में खिलती हैं ।
Sita came yesterday.
सीता कल आयी थी ।
The gymnast makes springing up to the bar look easy.
कसरतबाज डंडे के ऊपर से कूदने के कार्य को आसान बना देता है ।
It rained yesterday.
कल बारिश हुई थी ।
School will commence tomorrow.
विद्यालय कल से आरम्भ होगा ।
With a spring the cat reached the branch.
वह बिल्ली एक टहनी पर कूद गयी ।
I will come tomorrow.
मैं कल आऊँगा ।
The train stopped, and the child sprang for the door and in a twinkling was gone.
रेलगाड़ी के रुकते ही बच्चा दरवाजे से कूदकर रफूचक्कर हो गया ।
Sita loves the spring season.
सीता को वसन्त ऋतु अच्छी लगती है ।
He will e-mail us tomorrow.
वह हमें कल ईमेल करेगा ।

© Ankit Srivastava and Emily Bender, 2011. North American Computational Linguistics Olympiad, 2008 Round 1. This problem has been reproduced with the permission of the authors.

(10) Springing up Baby (2/2)

a. ऋतु	b. कलियाँ	c. कार्य	d. कूद	e. के
f. गया	g. टहनी	h. पर	i. बच्चा	j. बिल्ली
k. रफूचक्कर	l. वसन्त	m. सीता	n. से	o. है

10.1. In the above sentences, **spring** translates to two different Hindi words (in different sentences). Indicate which words from the following list are translations of **spring** (Circle the words.):

10.2. Which of the words you circled in B1 is the most likely translation of **spring** in the following sentence?

We always look forward to the **spring** holidays.

10.3. What is it about this sentence that suggests that the word you chose is the proper translations?:

10.4. In the Hindi sentences on the previous page, कल translates to two different English words (in different sentences). What are those words?

10.5. What is the most likely translation of कल in the following sentence?

अनामिका यहाँ कल आयी थी ।

10.6. What is it about this sentence that suggests that the word you chose is the proper translation?

13

(11) Reach for the Top (1/1)*****

The Ilocano language is one of the major languages of the Philippines, spoken by more than 8 million people. Today, it is written in the Roman alphabet, which was introduced by the Spanish, but before that, Ilocano was written in the *Baybayin* script. Baybayin (which literally means "spelling") was used to write many Philippine languages and was in use from the 14th to the 19th centuries.

11.1. Below are twelve Ilocano words written in Baybayin. Match them to their English translations, listed in scrambled order below.

{to look, is skipping for joy, is becoming a skeleton, to buy, various skeletons, various appearances, to reach the top, is looking, appearance, summit, happiness, skeleton}

11.2. Fill in the missing forms.

_____ (the/a) purchase

_____ is buying

11.3. Explain the reasoning behind your solutions to 11.1 and 11.2.

© Patrick Littell, 2011. North American Computational Linguistics Olympiad, 2008 Round 1. This problem has been reproduced with the permission of the author.

(12) Spare the Rod (1/2)***

An excerpt from a well known text is shown below. It is in two languages (X and Y) that are closely linguistically related to each other and also to English. However, the two versions are not perfect translations of one another.

Text in language X:

X1. Rödluvan: Men mormor, varför har du så stora ögon?
X2. "Mormor": Det är bara för att jag skall se dig bättre, mitt barn.
X3. Rödluvan: Men mormor, varför har du så stora öron?
X4. "Mormor": Det är bara för att jag skall höra dig bättre, mitt barn.
X5. Rödluvan: Men mormor, varför har du så stora tänder?
X6. "Mormor": Det är bara för att jag skall kunna äta upp dig!

(almost) the same text in language Y:

Y1. - Så store ører du har, bestemor, sa Rødhette.
Y2. - Det er fordi jeg skal kunne høre deg bedre, svarte ulven.
Y3. - Så store øyne du har, bestemor, sa Rødhette.
Y4. - Det er fordi jeg skal kunne se deg bedre, svarte ulven.
Y5. - Så store hender du har, bestemor, sa Rødhette.
Y6. - Det er fordi jeg skal kunne klemme deg bedre, svarte ulven.
Y7. - Så stor munn du har, bestemor, sa Rødhette.
Y8. - Det er fordi jeg skal kunne ete deg bedre, svarte ulven.

12.1. Translate sentences X1 and X2 into grammatical English using your own words and word order.

12.2. Align the eight sentences in text Y with the six sentences in text X by content. Which two sentences in Y remain unaligned?

_____	Y1	_____	Y5
_____	Y2	_____	Y6
_____	Y3	_____	Y7
_____	Y4	_____	Y8

12.3. Fill the leftmost column of the table on the next page. If you believe that a given word is not translated at all, use an X to indicate that.

12.4. Now, fill out the rightmost column of the table.

© Dragomir Radev, 2011. North American Computational Linguistics Olympiad, 2008 Round 1. This problem has been reproduced with the permission of the author.

(12) Spare the Rod (2/2)

Language X	Language Y	English
	så	
	store	
	ører	
	du	
	har	
	bestemor	
	sa	
	Rødhette	
	det	
	er	
	fordi	
	jeg	
	skal	
	kunne	
	høre	
	deg	
	bedre	
	svarte	
	ulven	
	øyne	
	se	
	hender	
	klemme	
	stor	
	munn	
	ete	

12.5. Explain the reasoning that you used to answer parts 12.1-12.4 in detail.

12.6. Say as much as you can about languages X and Y.

(13) A Fish Story (1/1)*****

Aymara is a South American language spoken by more then 2 million people in the area around Lake Titicaca, which, at 12,507 feet above sea level, is the highest navigable lake in the world. Among the speakers of Aymara are the *Uros*, a fishing people who live on artificial islands, woven from reeds, that float on the surface of Lake Titicaca.

13.1. Below, seven fishermen describe their catch. Who caught what?

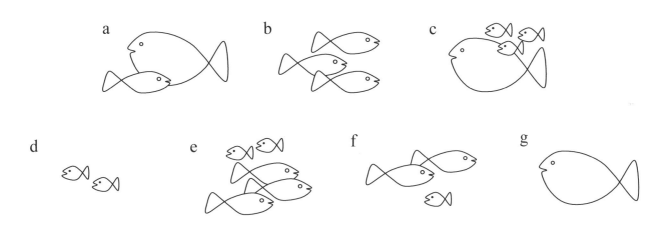

____ 1. *"Mä hach'a challwawa challwataxa."*

____ 2. *"Kimsa hach'a challwawa challwataxa."*

____ 3. *"Mä challwa mä hach'a challwampiwa challwataxa."*

____ 4. *"Mä hach'a challwa kimsa challwallampiwa challwataxa."*

____ 5. *"Paya challwallawa challwataxa."*

____ 6. *"Mä challwalla paya challwampiwa challwataxa."*

____ 7. *"Kimsa challwa paya challwallampiwa challwataxa."*

Also, watch out! *One of the fishermen is lying.*

13.2. Your daily catch is pictured to the right. Describe it in Aymara, and don't lie!

13.3. Describe your reasoning.

© Patrick Littell, 2011. North American Computational Linguistics Olympiad, 2008 Round 1. This problem has been reproduced with the permission of the author.

(14) Fakepapershelfmaker (1/2)***

In English, we can combine two nouns to get a compound noun, such as in 'mailbox' or 'sandcastle'. We can do this in Japanese as well, but just sticking the two words together isn't necessarily enough. Instead, the words themselves undergo predictable changes:

ikebana
'flower arranging'

ike   *hana*
'arrange'   'flower'

asagiri
'morning fog'

asa   *kiri*
'morning'   'fog'

hoshizora
'starry sky'

hoshi   *sora*
'star'   'sky'

Compound words can then be compounded again, creating compounds with three or more members. Study the diagrams below carefully. You'll notice that the order in which the compound is built affects both the meaning and the final form of the word.

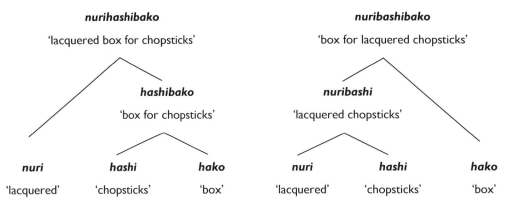

nurihashibako
'lacquered box for chopsticks'

hashibako
'box for chopsticks'

nuri   *hashi*   *hako*
'lacquered'   'chopsticks'   'box'

nuribashibako
'box for lacquered chopsticks'

nuribashi
'lacquered chopsticks'

nuri   *hashi*   *hako*
'lacquered'   'chopsticks'   'box'

14.1. The following is a list of several Japanese words with their English meanings. Use this word bank to write definitions of the Japanese compounds (a)-(f). Be very specific with how you phrase your definition. If your definition is ambiguous (has two meanings), it will not be counted.

sakura	cherry blossom	*kami*	paper	*nise*	fake
shiru	soup	*tana*	shelf	*tsukuri*	maker
iro	color(ed)	*tanuki*	raccoon	*hako*	box

(a) nisetanukijiru	
(b) nisedanukijiru	
(c) irogamibako	
(d) irokamibako	
(e) nisezakuradana	
(f) nisesakuradana	

© Willie Costello, 2011. North American Computational Linguistics Olympiad, 2008 Round 2. This problem has been reproduced with the permission of the author.

(14) Fakepapershelfmaker (2/2)

14.2. Match the following four-member Japanese compound words on the left with their English meanings on the right. (Some will require you to stretch your imagination a bit!) One of the Japanese words will correspond to two possible English meanings.

_____ (1) a fake (fraudulent) shelf-maker made of paper	(A) *nisegamidanadzukuri*
_____ (2) a maker of fake shelves for paper	(B) *nisekamitanadzukuri*
_____ (3) a fake (fraudulent) maker of shelves for paper	(C) *nisegamitanadzukuri*
_____ (4) a shelf-maker made of fake paper	(D) *nisekamidanadzukuri*
_____ (5) a maker of shelves for fake paper	

14.3. Explain your answers.

(15) Manam, I'm Anam (1/1)****

Manam Pile ("Manam Talk") is a Malayo-Polynesian language spoken on Manam Island off the coast of Papua New Guinea. Manam is one of the most active volcanoes in the world, and during violent eruptions, the population must be evacuated to the mainland.

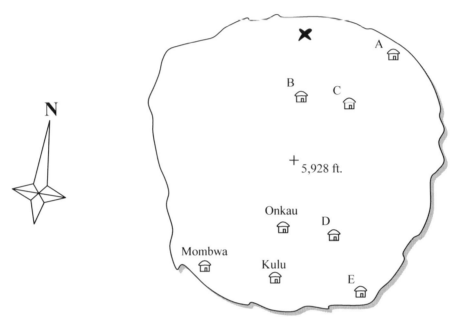

Below, a Manam islander describes the relative locations of the houses above.

1. *Onkau pera kana auta ieno, Kulu pera kana ilau ieno.*
2. *Mombwa pera kana ata ieno, Kulu pera kana awa ieno.*
3. *Tola pera kana auta ieno, Sala pera kana ilau ieno.*
4. *Sulung pera kana awa ieno, Tola pera kana ata ieno.*
5. *Sala pera kana awa ieno, Mombwa pera kana ata ieno.*
6. *Pita pera kana ilau ieno, Sulung pera kana auta ieno.*
7. *Sala pera kana awa ilau ieno, Onkau pera kana ata auta ieno.*
8. *Butokang pera kana awa auta ieno, Pita pera kana ata ilau ieno.*

15.1. Onkau's, Mombwa's, and Kulu's houses have already been located on the map above. Who lives in the other five houses?

15.2. Arongo is building his new house in the location marked with an X. In three Manam Pile sentences like the ones on the previous page, describe the location of Arongo's house in relation to the three closest houses.

15.3. Explain your answers.

© Patrick Littell, 2011. North American Computational Linguistics Olympiad, 2008 Round 2. This problem has been reproduced with the permission of the author.

(16) Thorny Stems (1/3)*

Wouldn't it be nice if your computer could understand English? In this problem, you will write down a small set of rules encoding one piece of your knowledge about English.

The problem you will approach is called "stemming." You know that "work", "working", "works", and "worked" are all forms of the same verb: "work". Similarly, "guesses" and "guess" are both forms of the same noun: "guess". Below you will find a list of pairs of a word and its stem, both nouns and verbs. Your goal is to write down a list of rules which is as short as possible, but covers all of the example pairs. You must also list exactly **one** exception for every rule which has one.

Example

> Rule 1: **If** a word ends in ss, **then** replace ss with ss to form the stem.
> Rule 2: **If** a word ends in s, **then** replace s with __ to form the stem.
> Rule 3: **Otherwise** the word is its own stem.

Let's look at how these rules will apply to a few examples. We always use only the first numbered rule that applies. For the word "work", Rules 1-2 do not apply, so we are left with Rule 3, "work" is its own stem. For the word "works", Rule 1 does not apply, but Rule 2 does, so the stem of "works" is formed by replacing the final "s" with nothing —i.e., deleting it, to form "work". Finally, for the word "grass", Rule 1 does apply, and so we replace "ss" with "ss", i.e., the word is unchanged, and then we stop.

Your goal is to write one list of rules which will apply to both the nouns and the verbs listed on the next page.

Exceptions

The rules you write will not always work. Any word for which your rules give the wrong stem is called an "exception". You will write down exceptions for your rules—an exception is written next to the first rule whose "if" part applies to it. For example, "guess" is not an exception to the rules above, since even though Rule 2 does not handle it, Rule 1 (which comes first) does. However, "cries" is an exception (these rules gives its stem as "crie" instead of "cry"), and it should be written next to Rule 2 as follows:

> **If** a word ends in ss, **then** replace ss with ss to form the stem. **Exception:** -none-
> **If** a word ends in s, **then** replace s with __ to form the stem. **Exception:** cries

Judging

Your score will be determined according to the following criteria:
> You should have rules to cover all the words in the list on the following page.
> You should use as few rules as you can.
> You should list an exception next to as many rules as you can.

© Eric Breck, 2011. North American Computational Linguistics Olympiad, 2008 Round 2. This problem has been reproduced with the permission of the author.

(16) Thorny Stems (2/3)

Words and stems

NOUNS

word	stem
backs	back
books	book
chiefs	chief
companies	company
duties	duty
dwarves	dwarf
grass	grass
moss	moss
potatoes	potato
presidents	president
roses	rose
shelves	shelf
stores	store
stapler	stapler
times	time
toe	toe
tomatoes	tomato
wives	wife

VERBS

word	stem
cried	cry
cries	cry
dished	dish
flies	fly
married	marry
killed	kill
listened	listen
ordered	order
resorts	resort
sailing	sail
tailing	tail
tell	tell

16.1. Your rules

Write your rules by filling in the blank rules on the following page. You do not need to use all the blank rules. Cross out any rules you do not use.

(16) Thorny Stems (3/3)

1. If a word ends in _____, then replace _____ with _____ to form the stem.
   Exception:
2. If a word ends in _____, then replace _____ with _____ to form the stem.
   Exception:
3. If a word ends in _____, then replace _____ with _____ to form the stem.
   Exception:
4. If a word ends in _____, then replace _____ with _____ to form the stem.
   Exception:
5. If a word ends in _____, then replace _____ with _____ to form the stem.
   Exception:
6. If a word ends in _____, then replace _____ with _____ to form the stem.
   Exception:
7. If a word ends in _____, then replace _____ with _____ to form the stem.
   Exception:
8. If a word ends in _____, then replace _____ with _____ to form the stem.
   Exception:
9. If a word ends in _____, then replace _____ with _____ to form the stem.
   Exception:
10. If a word ends in _____, then replace _____ with _____ to form the stem.
    Exception:
11. Otherwise the word is its own stem.

16.2. Explain your reasoning.

(17) aw-TOM-uh-tuh (1/2)***

Finite-state automata (FSA) are a type of abstract "machine" with many possible uses. One possible use is to guess what language a document (such as a webpage) is in. If we make an automaton that can distinguish between possible English words and impossible ones, and then give it a webpage with a bunch of words that are impossible in English (like "*aioaepa*" or "*ragaiiare*"), we can be pretty sure that the webpage isn't written in English. (Or, at least, isn't *entirely* written in English.)

Here is a finite state automaton that can distinguish between possible and impossible words in Rotokas, a language spoken on the island of Bougainville, off the coast of New Guinea. Rotokas has a very simple system of sounds and allows us to create a very small FSA.

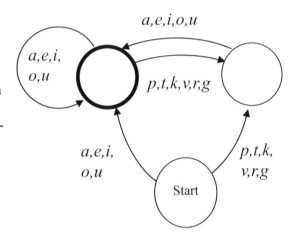

An FSA works like a board game. Choose a word, and place your pencil on the space marked "Start". Going through the letters of the word one at a time, move your pencil along the path marked with that letter. If the word ends and you're at a space marked with a thicker circle, the word succeeds: it's a possible Rotokas word! If the word ends and you're not at a thicker circle, or you're midway through the word and there's no path corresponding to the next letter, the word fails: it's *not* a possible Rotokas word!

Try it out with these possible and impossible words; the automaton should accept all the possible words and reject the impossible ones.

Possible Rotokas words		Impossible Rotokas words	
tauo	kareveiepa	grio	ouag
puraveva	ovokirovuia	ovgi	vonoka
avaopa	ouragaveva	gataap	oappa

17.1. Now, using the automaton above, put a check mark next to each possible Rotokas word:

____ iu	____ uente	____ voav
____ idau	____ urioo	____ uaia
____ oire	____ raorao	____ oratreopaveiepa

17.2. Actually, the system that people on Bougainville use to write Rotokas is a little more complicated

© Patrick Littell, 2011. North American Computational Linguistics Olympiad, 2008 Round 2. This problem has been reproduced with the permission of the author.

than the one we've presented here. In addition to the eleven letters above, the real Rotokas alphabet has a twelfth letter, S. This letter represents the sound "s" or "ts", which in Rotokas only occurs in very specific situations.

Below is a skeleton of an FSA for Rotokas with all the path labels removed and set to one side.

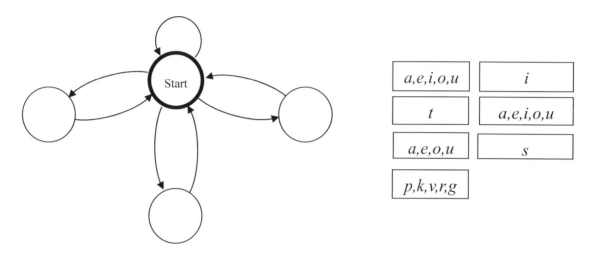

a,e,i,o,u	*i*
t	*a,e,i,o,u*
a,e,o,u	*s*
p,k,v,r,g	

Replace the path labels so that exactly half of the words below succeed and the other half fail.

oisio	*tiravau*	*saiuu*	*kotoe*
uasau	*utsa*	*sioparoia*	*parauos*
puapuata	*sisigarue*	*porouativeve*	*aasiia*

17.3. Why do T and S get their own paths? What is special about these letters?

(18) The Curragh of Kildare (1/1)****

And straight I will repair
To the Curragh of Kildare
For it's there I'll find tidings of my dear
[Irish Folk Song]

In Ireland, each place name has two versions with equal legal status—an English one and an Irish one. Below are some place-names in their two versions and translations of the Irish ones.

	English	Irish	Translation of Irish name
1	Glenamuckaduff	Gleann na Muice Duibhe	Valley of the Black Pig
2	Clonamully	Cluain an Mhullaigh	Meadow of the Summit
3	Buncurry	Bun an Churraigh	Base of the Marsh
4	Curraghmore	An Currach Mór	The Big Marsh
5	Annaghanoon	Eanach an Uain	Fen of the Lamb
6	Dunard	An Dún Ard	The High Fort
7	Bunagortbaun	Bun an Ghoirt Bháin	Base of the White Field
8	Gortnakilly	Gort na Cille	Field of the Church
9	Binbane	An Bhinn Bhán	The White Peak
10	Ballyknock	Baile an Chnoic	Town of the Hill
11	Ballynaparka	Baile na Páirce	Town of the Park
12	Kilcarn	Cill an Chairn	Church of the Mound
13	Killeshil	An Choill Íseal	The Low Wood
14	Clashbane	An Chlais Bhán	The White Pit
15	Bunbeg	An Bun Beag	The Small Base

Sometimes the English name is no more than a translation of the Irish one:

16	Blackabbey	An Mhainistir Dhubh
17	Bigpark	An Pháirc Mhór
18	Castlepark	Páirc an Chaisleáin
19	Woodland	Talamh na Coille

18.1. What would the Irish names of the following towns and villages be? Provide a translation for each one. If you think more than one Irish name could correspond to a given English name, give all of them:

	English	Irish	Translation of Irish name
20	Mullaghbane		
21	Killananny		
22	Knocknakillardy		
23	Gortnabinna		
24	Clashgortmore		
25	Killbeg		
26	Blackcastle		Black castle

© Todor Tchervenkov, 2011. North American Computational Linguistics Olympiad, 2008 Round 2. This problem has been reproduced with the permission of the author.

(19) Tzolk'in (1/2)****

Central to Mayan thought and religion was the concept of time, which was held to be cyclical and without beginning or end. Accurate reckoning of the day was highly important for ceremonial, political, and agricultural reasons, and to this end the Mayas kept several calendars of different length, all cycling simultaneously, while also keeping track of the exact number of days since August 11, 3114 BC.

The *tzolk'in* ritual and ceremonial calendar is the oldest and most important of these, and is not exclusively Mayan—it was shared by all of the ancient civilizations of Mexico, and predates Classical Mayan civilization by hundreds of years. It is also the main calendar to have survived, and is still in use today in some Mayan villages.

Given the conception of time as cyclical, it is appropriate that the *tzolk'in* has no identifiable beginning or end, but simply assigns names to days in an infinite loop. On the following page, we've taken a calendar for our August and September, but inserted the day names according to the *tzolk'in*.

19.1. What are the Mayan names of the days labeled *a* and *b* on the calendar? Draw the appropriate glyphs in the boxes below.

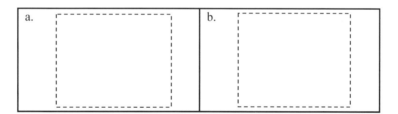

19.2. Where on the calendar would the following days fall? Write a *c* and a *d* on the appropriate days on the calendar.

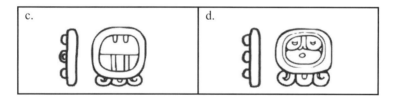

19.3. The two months shown are completely representative of the workings of the *tzolk'in*; there are no special sub-cycles, "leap" days, periods with fewer days than other periods, etc. Knowing that, *how often* does the following day occur?

© Patrick Littell and Erin Donnelly, 2011. North American Computational Linguistics Olympiad, 2008 Round 2. This problem has been reproduced with the permission of the authors.

(19) Tzolk'in (2/2)

AUGUST

SEPTEMBER

b

a

28

(20) The Whole Spectrum (1/3)****

Background

The sounds of human speech (and indeed all sounds) travel through the air in waves, some of which your ear detects as sounds. These waves can be analyzed (by a mathematical technique called "Fourier analysis") into combinations of basic ("sinusoidal") waves whose most important properties are "frequency" and "amplitude." One sound may comprise many such basic waves, and a basic wave of the same frequency or amplitude may appear in many sounds. Linguists sometimes display this analysis on a diagram called a spectrogram: the resulting sine waves' frequencies are plotted vertically (with greater amplitude indicated by darker points) and the time horizontally.

Data

A sequence of spectrograms produced using the computer software "Praat" is shown on the following pages. The first 12 are each labeled with an English word, which is shown in the spectrogram. The following words are given:

sash, lamb, knee, sheesh, soup, pang, loose, (the letter) e, mice, ice, coo, shine

The last four spectrograms each show one of the following eight words:

louse, lass, lease, lice, pass, ash, sheep, lack

Tasks

20.1. What words are shown in the last four spectrograms?

20.2. For each of the three most significant sounds in "sash," mark an interval corresponding to the duration of that sound. You should mark each interval by a horizontal line drawn above the spectrogram over all parts of the spectrogram affected by that sound.

20.3. Do the same for "lamb."

20.4. Explain your reasoning for part 20.1.

20.5. Discuss the correspondence between the English spellings of the given 12 words and their spectrograms. In particular, some letters' sounds affect longer intervals in the spectrograms than others do. Which letters and sounds affect the longest intervals? Do adjacent sounds' affected intervals overlap, and if so, how? Are there any letters that correspond to no interval at all, and which letters? Conversely, are there any distinct sounds on the spectrograms that correspond to no English letters, and where are those sounds?

© Adam Hesterberg, 2011. North American Computational Linguistics Olympiad, 2008 Round 2. This problem has been reproduced with the permission of the author.

(20) The Whole Spectrum (2/3)

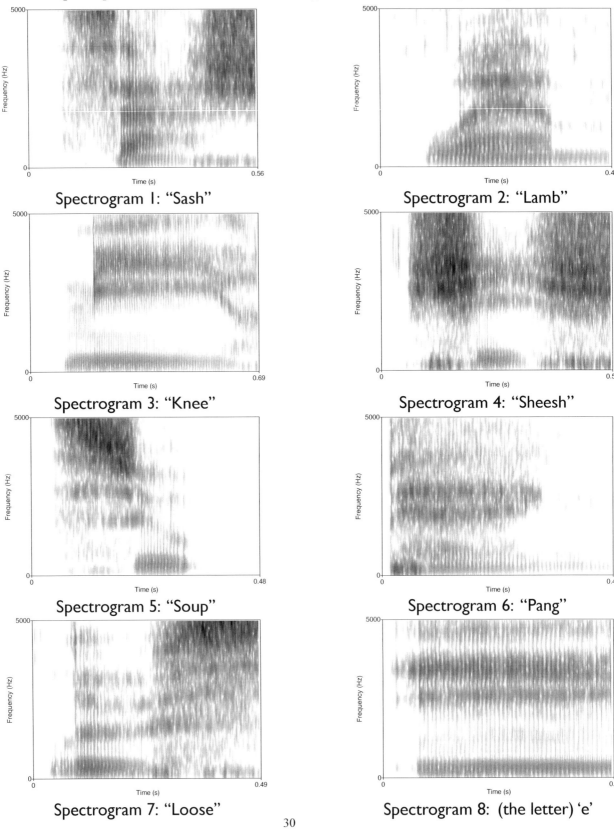

Spectrogram 1: "Sash"

Spectrogram 2: "Lamb"

Spectrogram 3: "Knee"

Spectrogram 4: "Sheesh"

Spectrogram 5: "Soup"

Spectrogram 6: "Pang"

Spectrogram 7: "Loose"

Spectrogram 8: (the letter) 'e'

30

(20) The Whole Spectrum (3/3)

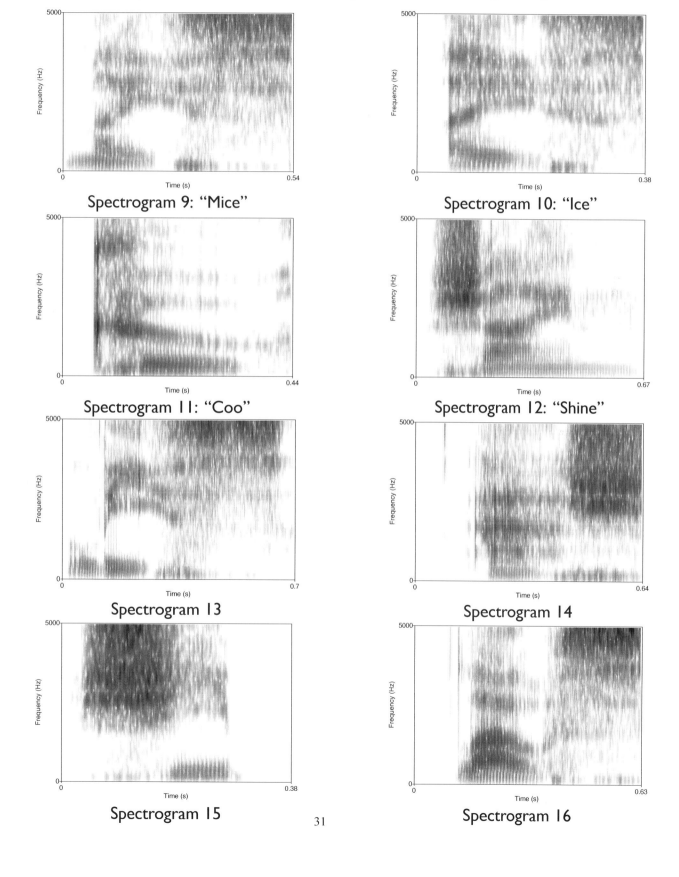

Spectrogram 9: "Mice"

Spectrogram 10: "Ice"

Spectrogram 11: "Coo"

Spectrogram 12: "Shine"

Spectrogram 13

Spectrogram 14

Spectrogram 15

Spectrogram 16

(21) Tenji Karaoke (1/1)**

Braille is a tactile writing system, based on a series of raised dots, that is widely used by the blind. It was invented in 1821 by Louis Braille to write French, but has since been adapted to many other languages. English, which uses the Roman alphabet just as French does, required very little adaptation, but languages that do not use the Roman alphabet, such as Japanese, Korean, or Chinese, are often organized in a very different manner!

To the right is a Japanese word written in the **tenji** ("dot characters") writing system. The large dots represent the raised bumps; the tiny dots represent empty positions.

21.1. The following *tenji* words represent **atari, haiku, katana, kimono, koi,** and **sake**. Which is which? You don't need to know either Japanese or Braille to figure it out; you'll find that the system is highly logical.

a. _____	b. _____
c. _____	d. _____
e. _____	f. _____

21.2. What are the following words?

g. _____	h. _____

21.3. Write the following words in *tenji* characters.

i. samurai	j. miso

© Patrick Littell, 2011. North American Computational Linguistics Olympiad, 2009 Round 1. This problem has been reproduced with the permission of the author.

(22) Nok-nok! (1/2)**

Christopher Robin is the most educated friend of Winnie-the-Pooh, and he can spell a lot of simple words, and even some long and delicate words, but unfortunately, he often spells them incorrectly. For example, he has helped Owl to write the following two notices on the door of Owl's residence at The Chestnuts:

| Ples ring if an rnser is reqird. |

| Plez cnoke if an rnsr is not reqid. |

Although Owl is very proud of these notices, he is also concerned that some of his friends may not under-stand them; in fact, even Owl himself finds the notices a bit confusing.

To help Christopher Robin with his spelling, Winnie-the-Pooh and Owl have bought him an electronic spelling tutor, which pronounces various words and asks the user to spell them. If the user makes a mistake, the tutor shows the correct spelling, along with a comment on the accuracy of the user's spelling; it uses four comments: *almost right*, *quite close*, *a bit confusing*, and *very confusing*. For instance, Christopher Robin has re-ceived the following feedback during his initial experiments with the tutor:

Spelling by Christopher Robin	Correct Spelling	Comment
flocinaucinihilipilification	loccinaucinihilipilification	almost right
owll	owl	almost right
pseudopseudohipoparathyroidism	pseudopseudohypoparathyroidism	almost right
ples	please	quite close
reqird	required	quite close
rnser	answer	quite close
antidisestablishmentaraniasm	antidisestablishmentarianism	quite close
wol	owl	quite close
humuhumunukunukuapuaua'a	humuhumunukunukuapua'a	quite close
plez	please	a bit confusing
cnoke	knock	a bit confusing
rnsr	answer	a bit confusing
reqid	required	a bit confusing
pneumonoultramicroscopiccilikovolka nokoniosis	pneumonoultramicroscopicsilicovolca nokoniosis	a bit confusing
mispeln	misspelling	very confusing
mestipenk	mistyping	very confusing

22.1. Your task is to determine how the tutor chooses its comments and give the appropriate comment for each of the six misspellings of the word *"typo"* found on the following page. You do not need to explain your answers; just indicate the right comments.

For each misspelling, put the "X" sign in the column with the appropriate comment. Please note that each row in the table must have *exactly one* X sign.

© Eugene Fink, 2011. North American Computational Linguistics Olympiad, 2009 Round 1. This problem has been reproduced with the permission of the author.

Misspelling of "typo"	Comment by the Tutor			
	Almost right	Quite close	A bit confusing	Very confusing
oooo				
opyt				
pyto				
typ				
typa				
typotypo				

As a side note, the dictionary definitions of the long and delicate words misspelled by Christopher Robin are as follows; these definitions are unrelated to the problem.

floccinaucinihilipilification: act or habit of estimating or describing something as worthless, or making something to be worthless by deprecation.

pseudopseudohypoparathyroidism: inherited disorder that closely simulates the symptoms, but not the consequences, of pseudohypoparathyroidism; thus, it has mild or no manifestations of hypoparathyroidism or tetanic convulsions.

antidisestablishmentarianism: nineteenth century movement in England opposed to the separation of church and state.

humuhumunukunukuapuaʻa: one of several species of triggerfish.

pneumonoultramicroscopicsilicovolcanokoniosis: lung disease caused by the inhalation of very fine silica dust, mostly found in volcanoes.

(23) Letters for Cuzco (1/1)***

Orthography design is the process of developing an alphabet and spelling rules for a language. A good orthography has several features:

* Given a spoken word, there's no question of how to spell it.
* Given a written word, there's no question of how to pronounce it.
* In the modern world, it's increasingly important that it be reasonably easy to type!

Quechua is spoken today by millions of people in Peru, Ecuador, and Bolivia, the descendants of the citizens of the Incan Empire. Quechua speakers are rapidly joining the Information Age, and both Google and Microsoft Windows now come in Quechua!

Like in English, there are more sounds in Quechua than there are letters on a keyboard, but there are ways around that. For example, we can assign one letter to multiple sounds, so long as a reader can always predict, from its position in the word or from other letters in the word, which sound is meant. So, if the sound [b] only ever occurs right after [m], and [p] never occurs right after [m], we can just write "p" for both, since you'll be able to predict from the previous letter whether "p" means [b] or [p].

This "phonemic principle" is the central principle of most orthographies, not just because it reduces letters, but also because our minds categorize sounds in the same way.

Here are 33 words in Cuzco Quechua as they are pronounced, but not necessarily as they are written. [q] and [χ] represent special sounds that don't occur in English.

awtu	car	qasi	free	seqay	to climb		
kanka	roasted	qatoχ	merchant	sikasika	caterpillar		
karu	far	qatuy	to barter	sipeχ	murderer		
kiru	teeth	qatisaχ	I will follow	sipiy	to kill		
kisa	nettle	qelqaχ	writer	soχtaral	sixty cents		
kisu	cheese	qelqay	to write	sunka	beard		
kunka	neck	qolqe	silver	toχra	ball of ash		
kusa	great	qosa	husband	uyariy	to listen		
layqa	witch	qosqo	Cuzco	uywaχ	caretaker		
oqe	spotted	saqey	to abandon	waleχ	a lot		
qasa	frost	saχsa	striped	weqaw	waist		

23.1. Show that we don't need separate letters for [q] and [χ].

23.2. Show that we can't represent [a] and [i] by the same letter.

23.3. Show that we can't represent [a] and [e] by the same letter.

23.4. Most modern Quechua orthographies get by with only three of the five vowels [a], [e], [i], [o], and [u]. Show how this is possible.

© Patrick Littell, 2011. North American Computational Linguistics Olympiad, 2009 Round 1. This problem has been reproduced with the permission of the author.

(24) You Will be Laughing (1/1)*****

The following Guaraní verb forms are listed along with their English translations.

N.	Guaraní	English translation
1	japyhyta	We will be catching
2	nohyvykõiri	He is not enjoying
3	ombokapu	He is shooting
4	pemomaitei	You are greeting
5	ndokarumo'ãi	He will not be eating
6	ndapevo'oima	You were not taking
7	napekororõmo'ãi	You will not be crying
8	noñe'ẽi	He is not talking
9	okororõ	He is crying
10	ndajajupirima	We were not waking up
11	ahyvykõima	I was enjoying
12	añe'ẽta	I will be talking
13	namomaiteiri	I am not greeting
14	japurahei	We are singing

24.1. Translate into English:

(a) *akaruma*   (b) *ojupita*   (c) *ndavo'omo'ãi*   (d) *napekororõi*   (e) *ndapyhyima*

24.2. Translate into Guaraní:

(f) *you are not shooting*   (g) *he is not singing*   (h) *we will be eating*   (i) *I will not be singing*

Note: "you" is always plural in the sentences above. A squiggle over a vowel indicates that it is nasal (pronounced partly through the nose). The letter *ñ* is pronounced like the sound in the middle of "piñata" or "onion". The letter *y* is pronounced like the "u" in "cut". The letter *j* and the apostrophe (') are specific consonants.

Guaraní is one of the official languages (along with Spanish) of Paraguay, where it is spoken by 94% of the population.

© Bozhidar Bozhanov, 2011. North American Computational Linguistics Olympiad, 2009 Round 1. This problem has been reproduced with the permission of the author.

(25) Summer Eyes (1/2)*****

Below are two news stories, each of which has had three sentences automatically selected as a summary by a computer, based on a number of criteria. The criteria are the same for each story. Within each story, some scores may depend on other sentences. Below each story, a change has been proposed to one of the sentences.

25.1. Rescore the sentences after the change, using the same criteria: in each score box, either write the appropriate new score if it's different from the old one, or LEAVE IT BLANK IF IT WOULD BE UNCHANGED. For instance, a correctly formatted (but wrong) possible answer for the first sentence is:

I	X	3.4	0	I	4	0	-1	7.4	Taiwan authorities say a powerful earthquake has struck the southeastern part of the island.
		1.7	3			-1	2	0.7	

25.2. For each story, put the symbol X in exactly three of the boxes in the first column, the ones corresponding to the sentences in the new summary.

25.3: Give the added sentence in the second story scores according to the same criteria.

Story 1 input:

Powerful earthquake strikes Taiwan

Sentence Number		Criteria						Total score	Sentence
		1st	2nd	3rd	4th	5th	6th		
1	X	3.4	0	I	4	0	-1	7.4	Taiwan authorities say a powerful earthquake has struck the south-eastern part of the island.
2		2.3	0	0	0	0	-2	0.3	There were no immediate reports of damages or injuries from the Tuesday morning quake, authorities said.
3	X	1.2	I	2	2	2	-1	7.2	The Taiwan Central Weather Bureau says the magnitude 6.0 quake struck just offshore, near a sparsely populated area about 20 miles (30 kilometers) north of the city of Taidung.
4		0.1	2	I	0	I	-1	3.1	However, the U.S. Geological Survey says the quake had a magnitude of 5.2.
5	X	0.0	3	I	0	I	-1	4.0	Buildings shook in Taipei about 90 miles (150 kilometers) to the north-west of the epicenter.

Story 1 output: An "extractive summary" consisting of sentences 1, 3, and 5.
Story 1 proposed change: Add "in Taipei" between "damages or injuries" and "from" in sentence 2.

© Dragomir Radev and Adam Hesterberg, 2011. North American Computational Linguistics Olympiad, 2009 Round 1. This problem has been reproduced with the permission of the authors.

(25) Summer Eyes (2/2)

Story 2 input:

Sentence Number	Criteria						Total score	Sentence
	1st	2nd	3rd	4th	5th	6th		
1 X	3.8	0	1	7	0	-3	8.8	Mexico's interior minister has died in a plane crash, after the small aircraft he was travelling in plummeted into rush hour traffic in the nation's capital.
2	2.7	0	1	1	1	-1	4.7	He was one of the architects of conservative Felipe Calderón's 2006 election victory.
3	1.6	0	2	1	1	-2	3.6	Calderón described Mouriño as "a compatriot who worked for the service of his county."
4	0.5	0	1	3	1	-1	4.5	Jose Luis Santiago Vasconcelos, the deputy attorney-general until recently and a key player for years in the war on drug cartels, also died in the crash.
5 X	0.4	0	3	3	3	-4	5.4	Communications minister Luis Tellez said everything pointed to the crash being an accident but Jorge Lara, vice-president of a national civil aviation rescue committee, told Reuters "It could have been anything, from mechanical failure to sabotage."
6	0.3	0	1	3	0	-4	0.3	A colleague of Lara at the scene said it appeared something happened to the plane in the air and it nosedived into the ground.
7	0.2	1	0	0	0	-1	0.2	Surrounding buildings were not damaged.
8	0.1	2	2	2	2	-3	5.1	Newspaper El Universal reported an air traffic controller as saying the aircraft had been coming in to land at Mexico City's airport when it hit the ground between tall office buildings.
9 X	0.0	3	2	4	1	-3	7.0	Tellez said there was no contact with the plane, which had been returning from a trip to the central city of San Luis Potosí, in the moments before the crash.

Table title: **Interior minister of Mexico dies in plane crash that killed eight**

Story 2 output: An "extractive summary" consisting of sentences 1, 5, and 9.

Story 2 proposed change: Add the following sentence between the current second and third sentences:

n/a	n/a	n/a	n/a	n/a	n/a	n/a	n/a	Seven other people were killed and 40 injured when the government jet smashed into the streets of Mexico City yesterday, setting several cars ablaze, Reuters reported.
3								

(26) Help My Camera! (1/1)**

In the following dialogues, the computer is misunderstanding the human, because it is misinterpreting certain words or phrases:

Example 1

> **Human**: There's this restaurant on Bancroft that's supposed to be really good that I heard about from my mother. Can you help me find it?
> **Computer**: Where did you last see your mother?

Example 2

> **Human**: My friend is looking for information about on-line movie databases. What should I tell him?
> **Computer**: You can tell movie databases about movies that you have seen.

Example 3

> **Human**: My parents are having a hard time choosing a new digital camera. How can I help them?
> **Computer**: I'm afraid I don't understand your question. People don't help cameras.

26.1. What are the words (or phrases) that the computer is misinterpreting?

Ex1: _____ Ex2: _____ Ex3: _____

26.2. What rule is the computer using to interpret those words (or phrases)?

26.3. Give a better rule that would make the computer interpret the words (or phrases) correctly in these examples.

© Emily Bender, 2011. North American Computational Linguistics Olympiad, 2009 Round 1. This problem has been reproduced with the permission of the author.

(27) Sk8 Parsr (1/3)**

Languages are everywhere... even in places where you don't expect them.

Consider the "combo rules" of *P-Little's Triple-I XTreem Hyp0th3tica7 Sk8boarding Game*. In it, players press a series of buttons (left, right, down, up, circle, triangle, square, and X) to make their on-screen avatar perform skateboard tricks that illustrate pro boarder P-Little's "Triple-I" philosophy of Insane, Ill-Advised, and Impossible According to the Laws of Physics. Underneath, the game is using the methods of computational linguistics to turn this "little language" of button presses into tricks and combos. The game uses a simple **shift-reduce parser** to parse button "words" into combo "sentences". As each button-press comes in, the corresponding symbols are placed, in order, in a *buffer* (that is, temporary storage space).

1.	↑
2.	↑ ←
3.	↑ ← ▢
4.	↑ ← ▢ ⊗

If, at any point, the *rightmost* symbols in this buffer match any of the patterns on the next page, they are removed and replaced with a new symbol indicating a combo. So, since ▢ ⊗ corresponds to an "ollie", we replace it with the new symbol **Ollie**.

5.	↑ ← **Ollie**
6.	↑ ← **Ollie** ▢
7.	↑ ← **Ollie** ▢ ▢
8.	↑ ← **Ollie** ▢ ▢ ⊗
9.	↑ ← **Ollie** ▢ **Ollie**

More complex combos can then be built out of simpler combos. You see in the fifth rule on the next page that **Ollie** and **Nollie** can be joined by ▢ to make a new combo. There are also **rule schemas** that can create new combos out of *any* kind of combo. The tenth rule on the next page says that *any* combo (represented by α), whether it's an Ollie or an Inverted-360-Kickflip, can be joined with itself by a ▢ to make a Double combo:

10.	↑ ← **Double-Ollie**

© Patrick Littell, 2011. North American Computational Linguistics Olympiad, 2009 Round 2. This problem has been reproduced with the permission of the author.

The chart of shift-replace rules is given below… but with some holes in it.

If the right side of the input matches…		… replace it with …
← ↑ ⬠	⟹	**Backside-180**
	⟹	**Frontside-180**
⬚ ⊗	⟹	**Ollie**
	⟹	**Nollie**
Nollie ⬚ Ollie	⟹	_____
↓ ↓	⟹	**Crouch**
	⟹	**Backside-360**
	⟹	**360-Kickflip**
	⟹	_____
α ⬚ α	⟹	**Double-α**
Double-α ⬚ α	⟹	**Triple-α**
Double-α ⬚ Double-α	⟹	**Quadruple-α**
_____	⟹	**Atomic-α**

Complex combos can get pretty involved. Here are a few combos from the manual to give you an idea:

Inverted-Nollie: ↓⊗▢↑
Double-Inverted-Woolie: ↓⊗○▢○⊗↑▢↓⊗○▢○⊗↑
Inverted-Triple-Backside-180:   ↓←↑△▢←↑△▢←↑△↑
Atomic-Double-Frontside-180:   →↓○▢→↓○▢↓→↓○▢→↓○↑
Inverted-Backside-360:   ↓←↑△→↓○↑
Triple-360-Kickflip: ↓↓←↑△→↓○▢↓↓←↑△→↓○▢↓↓←↑△→↓○

27.1. How would you perform an "Inverted-Atomic-Backside-360"?

27.2. How about an "Atomic-Atomic-Ollie"?

27.3. The shift-reduce rules given above are incomplete. Using the descriptions of advanced combos in the manual, can you fill in the missing pieces? State them as concisely as possible.

27.4. During playtesting, the testers discover that even though combos like "Quadruple-Ollie" and "Quadruple-Inverted-Woolie" are listed in the manual, the game can never actually recognize any Quadruple combo that the player performs. Why not? How could you fix the game so that it can?

27.5. What other types of combinations of the listed combos can never actually be pulled off by the player, and why not?

(28) Linear Combinations (1/3)***

The script Linear B, deciphered by the architect and amateur epigrapher Michael Ventris in 1953, was used to write Mycenean Greek around the 15th century BCE. Linear B tablets, all of which were accounting records, have been found both on Crete and at various Mycenaean sites on the Greek mainland.

Linear B isn't perfectly suited for Greek; it is an adaptation of another script (Linear A) that was used to write a language about which very little is known. Linear A/B didn't distinguish /l/ and /r/, nor did it have a way to distinguish similar triples of sounds like /ba/, /pa/, and /pʰa/ (which were distinct sounds in Greek), and apparently could only write sequences of V or CV syllables so that a syllable in a Greek word like kʰrusos 'gold' had to be broken up as something like ku-ru-so. Here V stands for vowel and C stands for consonant. The superscript ʰ is used to indicate aspiration.

You will now be asked to decipher a portion of the Linear B symbol set.

The map below shows the approximate locations of a number of ancient Cretan towns: the spellings reflect their probable pronunciation in Mycenaean Greek (not their pronunciation in Modern Greek). Note that we do not know the location of Kuprios; also, Tulisos and Kunari are two different places. Most of these names have stayed more or less the same up until the present day. However, one of the names on the map (a "distractor") is not the name that was used in Mycenaean times.

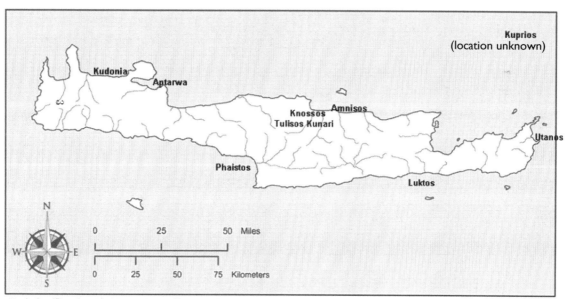

Map by Tom Elliott. Copyright 2003, Ancient World Mapping Center

This item may be reproduced and redistributed freely for non-profit, personal or educational use only. For all other uses, you must obtain prior, written permission from the copyright holder(s). The authorship, copyright and redistribution notices may not be removed from the map or altered.

© Richard Sproat, 2011. North American Computational Linguistics Olympiad, 2009 Round 2. This problem has been reproduced with the permission of the author.

(28) Linear Combinations (2/3)

28.1. Given the spellings of these names in Linear B, can you figure out which is which?

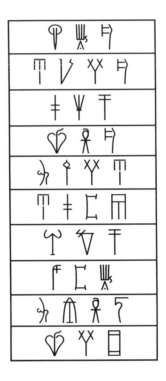

28.2. Identify the distractor mentioned on the previous page. What was the approximate Mycenaean pronunciation, given the Linear B spelling? Since one of the symbols used there only occurs in that name in this set, we will even give you a hint: that symbol represents *ja* (pronounced *ya*). Note that if you solve all the others, you will be able to read this name.

(28) Linear Combinations (3/3)

28.3. Write the most likely pronunciation of each Linear B symbol at right.

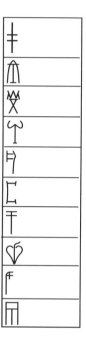

28.4. What are the probable pronunciations of the following words?

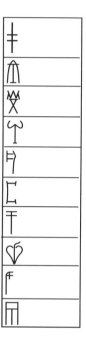	'girl'	
	'all'	
	'this'	
	'Cumin'	
	'linen'	

(29) Easy Pieces (I/I)*****

Below are phrases in Bulgarian and their translations into English:

	Bulgarian phrase	**English translation**
1	červẹni yạbəlki	red apples
2	kọsteni iglị	bone needles
3	studẹni napịtki	cold drinks
4	dosạdni decạ	annoying children
5	obiknovẹn čovẹk	ordinary person
6	gnẹvni dụmi	angry words
7	červẹn plod	red fruit
8	lẹnen plat	linen fabric
9	sọčni plodovẹ	juicy fruits
10	kọžni zabolyạvaniya	skin diseases
11	gnẹven sədiyạ	angry judge
12	rịbeni kyuftẹta	fish croquettes (type of food)
13	kirpịčeni kə̣šti	adobe houses
14	kọženi rəkavịci	leather gloves
15	lẹsen ịzpit	easy exam
16	cẹnni knịgi	precious books
17	sọčen grẹypfrut	juicy grapefruit
18	cẹnen predmẹt	precious object

Note: Bulgarian is written in the Cyrillic alphabet. Here it is given in transcription, where č, š, ž, and c stand for specific consonants of the Bulgarian language and ə is a vowel. Stressed vowels are marked with a dot underneath them. For words with only one vowel, stress is not marked.

29.1. Three rules govern the formation of the plural of the adjectives. What are they?

29.2. Apply the rules from part 1 and fill in the gaps in the following table:

	Bulgarian phrase	**English translation**
19	... procedụri	ordinary procedures
20	... urọci	easy lessons
21	... restorạnti	fish restaurants
22	... zabolyạvaniya	bone diseases
23	... čaršạfi	linen sheets

© Todor Tchervenkov, 2011. North American Computational Linguistics Olympiad, 2009 Round 2. This problem has been reproduced with the permission of the author.

(30) Hypo-Hmong-driac (1/1)***

The meanings of words may be related in various ways. One of these relations is called *hyponymy*. A word is a *hyponym* of another word if the things or events to which the first word can refer are a subset of the things or events to which the second word can refer. Thus, *spaniel* is a hyponym of *dog* (every spaniel is a dog), *crimson* is a hyponym of *red* (anything that is crimson is red), and *devour* is a hyponym of *eat* (since you cannot devour something without eating it).

Below, you are given a number of words in Mong Leng, also known as Green Hmong (a language of Southern China, Laos, Thailand, and Vietnam) that are related by hyponymy. The subset symbol ⊂ is used here to mean "are hyponyms of." A, B ⊂ C would mean that both A and B are hyponyms of C. Some of the items are simple words, consisting of a single root; others are compound words, made by combining two or more roots. You are also provided with a list of English translations of these words. Write the number for the Hmong word next to its English translation.

```
                    (1) sab, (2) ntswg ⊂ (3) sab-ntswg
                    (4) dlej, (5) cawv ⊂ (6) dlej-cawv
                    (7) nyaj, (8) txaj ⊂ (9) nyaj-txaj
                   (10) dlev, (11) npua ⊂ (12) dlev-npua
                   (13) qab,  (11) npua ⊂ (14) qab-npua
         (15) nyuj-twm, (14) qab-npua ⊂ (16) qab-npua-nyuj-twm
                       (17) nqaj-nyuj ⊂ (18) nqaj
                       (19) maum-npua ⊂ (20) maum
                         (21) sab-twm ⊂ (1) sab
          (22) lug-txaj, (23) lug-dlev-npua ⊂ (24) lug
 (25) poob-sab, (26) poob-nyaj, (27) poob-dlej ⊂ (28) poob
  (29) mob-sab, (30) mob-hlwb, (31) mob-ntswg ⊂ (32) mob
```

Note that some Hmong words occur more than once, but are always assigned the same number.

___ be lost	___ lose money ("silver")
___ beef	___ lungs
___ beverage	___ money
___ bovine[1] livestock	___ small, non-bovine livestock
___ chicken (the animal)	___ pig (the animal)
___ dog (the animal)	___ poetic genre ("money-language")
___ filthy animals; filth	___ silver
___ filthy language	___ suffer from a headache ("brain-ache")
___ flesh; meat	___ suffer from grief ("liver-ache")
___ hurt	___ suffer from lung disease ("lung-ache")
___ internal organs; soul	___ water
___ language	___ water-buffalo liver
___ liver (the organ)	___ wealth
___ livestock	___ whisky
___ lose heart ("liver"); lose one's wits; panic	___ young female
___ lose life to water; drown	___ young sow[2]

[1] Bovines are a group of large hooved mammals including cattle, water buffalo, bison, and yaks.
[2] A sow is a female pig.

© David Mortensen, 2011. North American Computational Linguistics Olympiad, 2009 Round 2. This problem has been reproduced with the permission of the author.

(31) The Gerbil Arrived (1/1)*

Below are given Dyirbal sentences and their English translations.

	Dyirbal	English
1	ŋinda bayi ñalŋga walmbin.	You woke the boy.
2	bayi ŋuma baŋgul ñalŋgaŋgu buṛan.	The boy saw the father.
3	ŋađa banagañu.	I returned.
4	bayi yuṛi baniñu.	The kangaroo came.
5	ŋađa bayi yaṛa buṛan.	I saw the man.
6	bayi ñalŋga baŋgul yaṛaŋgu ñiman.	The man caught the boy.
7	bayi ŋuma ñinañu.	The father sat.

Note: đ, ñ, ŋ and ṛ are specific consonants. Dyirbal (pronounced "jirble") is from the Pama-Nyungan language family, and was spoken in Queensland, Australia. It is practically extinct.

31.1. How are Dyirbal words and sentences formed? This is an important part of the problem's solution.

31.2. Give the English translations for these sentences.

bayi ñalŋga banagañu.
bayi yaṛa baŋgul yuṛiŋgu walmbin.
ŋinda bayi yuṛi buṛan .

31.3. Give Dyirbal translations for these sentences.

You sat.
I caught the kangaroo.
The father woke the man

© Bozhidar Bozhanov, 2011. North American Computational Linguistics Olympiad, 2009 Round 2. This problem has been reproduced with the permission of the author.

(32) Yak, Du, Dray (1/2)***

Consider the following arithmetic expression in Kuvi (a language from southeastern India):

$$(PA{:}SA \times SA{:}RI) + (NO{:} \times A{:}TA) = (PA{:}SA \times DOS) + (SO{:} \times SA{:}TA)$$

The "x" symbol above is the multiplication symbol. The ":" symbol denotes a long vowel. All seven words in the expression above are distinct integers from 1 to 10.

Your task is to order the following expressions by value (in increasing order). No two expressions have the same value.

(A)	**A:TA – RINDI**	(in Kuvi)
(B)	**DHJETË – GJASHTË**	(in Albanian)
(C)	**HASHT – SE**	(in Farsi)
(D)	**SÉ – CÚIG**	(in Irish)
(E)	**CHA – CHA:R**	(in Nepali)
(F)	**NAYN – EYNS**	(in Yiddish)
(G)	**DAS – TIN**	(in Pengo)
(H)	**AŠTUONI – PENKI**	(in Lithuanian)

The "–" symbol above is a minus. The eight expressions correspond to eight distinct positive integers.

As you can easily guess, solving this problem with only the information given above is impossible. However, we have some additional information that we can use. Below, you can see the numbers from 1 to 10 in a few languages. Each line lists all these numbers in the given language.

Nepali: **A:T, CHA, CHA:R, DAS, DUI, EK, NAU, PA:NCH, SA:T, TIN**
Pengo: **AT, CAR, CO, DAS, NOV, PÃC, RI, RO, SAT, TIN**
Farsi: **CHAHA:R, DAH, DO, HAFT, HASHT, NOH, PANJ, SE, SHESH, YAK**
Lithuanian: **AŠTUONI, DEŠIMT, DEVYNI, DU, KETURI, PENKI, SEPTYNI, ŠEŠI, TRYS, VIENAS**
Albanian: **DHJETË, DY, GJASHTË, KATËR, NËNTË, NJË, PESË, SHTATË, TETË, TRE**
Yiddish: **AKHT, DRAY, EYNS, FINF, FIR, NAYN, TSEN, TSVEY, ZEKS, ZIBN**
Irish: **AON, CEATHAIR, CÚIG, DEICH, DÓ, NAOI, OCHT, SÉ, SEACHT, TRÍ**

Note that on each row **above**, the numbers are sorted **alphabetically** (using their Latin transcriptions) and **not numerically**. The languages themselves are sorted geographically from East to West. Pengo and Kuvi are from the Dravidian family of languages. The other languages used in this problem belong to the Indo-European language family. The Dravidian languages use several number words of Indo-European origin.

Next you also have access to the following lists of numbers (this time sorted **numerically** from 1 to 10 on each line):
German: eins, zwei, drei, vier, fünf, sechs, sieben, acht, neun, zehn
Latin: unus, duo, tres, quattuor, quinque, sex, septem, octo, novem, decem
Ancient Greek: en, duo, tria, tettara, pente, hex, hepta, octo, ennea, deca

© Dragomir Radev, 2011. North American Computational Linguistics Olympiad, 2009 Round 2. This problem has been reproduced with the permission of the author.

(32) Yak, Du, Dray (2/2)

32.1. Fill in the blanks in the table below with the letters A—H, as appropriate. One cell should remain blank. (It should be obvious why there are no 0 or 10 columns).

1	2	3	4	5	6	7	8	9

32.2. Explain (concisely, yet precisely) the key insights that you used in solving this problem.

(33) Orwellspeak (1/3)***

Part 1. Opposites Attract

Here is a fragment of an English grammar. If you speak according to this grammar, you will utter sentences like `happy people love charming bad people.`

1.	**Sentence**	→	**NounPhrase + Verb + NounPhrase**
2.	**NounPhrase**	→	**Noun**
3.	**NounPhrase**	→	**Adjective + NounPhrase**
4.	**Noun**	→	`people`
5.	**Verb**	→	`love`
6.	**Adjective**	→	`good`
7.	**Adjective**	→	`charming`
8.	**Adjective**	→	`happy`
9.	**Adjective**	→	`bad`
10.	**Adjective**	→	`obnoxious`
11.	**Adjective**	→	`unhappy`

What do the above grammar rules mean? For example,
- Rule 1 says that to utter a **Sentence**, one must utter a **NounPhrase**, then a **Verb**, then a **NounPhrase.**
- Rules 2-3 offer two choices for uttering a **NounPhrase**: one may either utter a **Noun**, or utter an **Adjective** followed by another **NounPhrase.**
- Rules 6-11 offer several choices of **Adjective.**

Now, keep in mind that **opposites attract**. So, it is true that
- `good people love bad people`
- `good happy people love obnoxious people`
- `happy charming people love unhappy obnoxious bad unhappy unhappy people`

and also vice-versa,
- `bad people love good people`
- `obnoxious people love good happy people`
- `unhappy obnoxious bad unhappy unhappy people love happy charming people`

© Jason Eisner, 2011. North American Computational Linguistics Olympiad, 2009 Round 2. This problem has been reproduced with the permission of the author.

(33) Orwellspeak (2/3)

But it is false that
- `good people love good people`
- `obnoxious people love bad unhappy people`
- `people love good people`

33.1. Following the example of the totalitarian government in George Orwell's famous book *1984*, we would like you to revise the grammar of English so that it does not permit false **Sentences**.[1] The above grammar permits many **Sentences**. Your revised grammar should permit only a subset of these, using the same notation. It should systematically enforce the principle that opposites (and only opposites) attract. For example, it should be possible to utter the true example **Sentences** above, but not the false ones. It should also be impossible to discuss `charming bad people` or `unhappy good people`. (Such people pose intolerable problems for our moral philosophy, and their situations will be corrected forthwith.)

Please show your revisions directly on the grammar on the previous page, using the same notation, by adding new rules and by crossing out or otherwise modifying some of the old rules.

Part 2. Censorship

Consider again the setting of the previous problem ("Opposites Attract"). You can do this problem even if you did not solve the previous problem.

In an orderly society, only true, well-formed sentences should be uttered. Thus, our censors should detect illegal utterances like
- `good people love happy people` (which is false since only opposites attract)
- `bad bad bad` (which is nonsense and possibly a subversive code)
- `good charming people love` (which is not a complete sentence)

To be precise, if an utterance is a possible **Sentence** under the revised grammar that you were asked to write in the previous problem, then it is legal. Otherwise it is illegal and must be censored.

A vendor of censorship software has proposed a faster solution that does not use a grammar. Their device censors an utterance if and only if it contains at least one **bad phrase**. Each bad phrase in the device's memory is a sequence of **up to 4** adjacent words.

An input utterance would be presented in the form

`START good people love obnoxious happy END`

---

[1] "It was intended that when Newspeak had been adopted once and for all and Oldspeak forgotten, a heretical thought—that is, a thought diverging from the principles of [the Party]—should be literally unthinkable, at least so far as thought is dependent on words. Its vocabulary was so constructed as to give exact and often very subtle expression to every meaning that a Party member could properly wish to express, while excluding all other meaning . . . " —from "The Principles of Newspeak", an appendix to *1984* by G. Orwell, 1948.

(33) Orwellspeak (3/3)

Input utterances may be of any length. You may assume that they begin with START and end with END, and that in between, they use only words from the 8-word vocabulary

{people, love, good, charming, happy, bad, obnoxious, unhappy}.

33.2. The vendor's device has been carefully constructed to censor as many illegal utterances as possible while not censoring any legal ones. What is the shortest possible list of bad phrases that will do this? Write out a summary of the phrases on the list, and be sure to give the total number of phrases. For example, the list might include the 2-word bad phrase people charming, since this can never occur in a legal sentence. To indicate that there are 6 bad phrases of this general form, your summary list might include a line

people **Adjective** (6)

or if you prefer,

Noun Adjective (6)

    (Hint: The vocabulary consists of 1 **Noun**, 1 **Verb**, 3 positive **Adjective**s, and 3 negative **Adjective**s. A bad phrase may contain any of these words, and may also contain START and/or END. Remember that a bad phrase may consist of UP TO 4 adjacent words.)

33.3. Does the resulting device ever fail to censor an illegal utterance? If so, give an example.

33.4. Suppose the government tightens its grip, and requires that the vendor modify its machine to censor ALL illegal utterances (even if this means censoring some legal ones as well). What is the shortest possible list of bad phrases that meets this new requirement?

(34) Anishinaabemowin (1/2)**

Anishinaabemowin, also known as Ojibwa, Ojibwe, or Chippewa, is among the most-spoken American Indian languages in North America today. It is a member of the Algonquian family of languages, which were the first languages to be encountered by English settlers in North America. Coming across new and strange plants and animals, the settlers had to borrow words for them, so many words in English—including "moose", "raccoon", "opossum", "squash", and many others—originally come from Algonquian languages!

A few varieties of Anishinaabemowin, spoken in Michigan and Ontario, sound very different from other varieties. These dialects, called "Nishnaabemwin" by their speakers, have undergone a startling sound change in the last fifty years or so. By comparing Nishnaabemwin words to those of a closely related dialect, Minnesota Ojibwe, you can discover what happened, and even predict Nishnaabemwin words from their Minnesota Ojibwe relatives.

34.1. Can you discover an algorithm (i.e., a step-by-step procedure) for turning Minnesota Ojibwe words into Nishnaabemwin words? Write in the missing Nishnaabemwin forms in the table below.

A bar above a vowel, as in "ā", indicates that the vowel is long.

Minnesota Ojibwe	Nishnaabemwin	English
amik	mik	beaver
mitig	mtig	tree
okosimān	kosmān	pumpkin
makizinan	mkiznan	moccasins
niwābamigonān	nwābmignān	he or she sees us
makwa		bear
adōpowin		able

34.2. Now consider the following data. You will need to modify your algorithm slightly to handle these forms.

Minnesota Ojibwe	Nishnaabemwin	English
mōz	mōz	moose
ginebig	gnebig	snake
manidō	mnidō	Manitou, spirit
mitigwāb		bow
opwāgan		pipe

© Patrick Littell, 2011. This problem has been reproduced with the permission of the author.

(34) Anishinaabemowin (2/2)

34.3. Finally, here are a few more forms. Can your algorithm be modified to handle these as well? If your algorithm is correct, it should work for all the forms on this page. Now that you've seen all of the data, what is the algorithm you've devised? Write out a step-by-step procedure for getting a Nishnaabemwin word from its Minnesota Ojibwe relative.

Minnesota Ojibwe	Nishnaabemwin	English
jīmān	jīmān	"canoe"
ēsibanag	ēsbanag	"raccoons"
aninātig	ninātig	"maple tree"
anishinābēmowin	nishnābēmwin	"Indian language"
gichi-mōkomān	gchi-mōkmān	"American"
mīgwan		"feather"
gwīwizens		"boy"
nimishōmis		"my grandfather"

(35) Handwriting Recognition (1/1)[*]

A very bad handwriting recognition program recently interpreted a high school student's note providing a 10-word excuse for being late to class. The output is below.

lie	charm	code	soil	rout	wake	he	us	this	moving
my	solemn	circle	did	hot	make	I'll	is	taxi	having
guy	clam	shute	raid	riot	sale	me	ugh	thai	running
bye	beam	clock	risk	not	wane	be	up	tear	morning
	alarm	visit	must			see			loving
	dream								

35.1. Determine what the student's excuse was.

35.2. Explain how you could make the handwriting recognition program produce an output that is closer to what the student actually meant to write.

© Thomas Payne, 2011. This problem has been reproduced with the permission of the author.

(36) Hawaiian (1/1)**

Hawaiian is a Polynesian language, spoken fluently by about 2000 people.

The following Hawaiian sentences, with their English translations, are about a girl named Mele and a boy named Keone:

1. He has seven elder brothers.	*Ehiku ona kaikuaana.*
2. Mele has one brother.	*Ekahi o Mele kaikunane.*
3. Keone has one younger brother.	*Ekahi o Keone kaikaina.*
4. Mele has no elder sisters.	*Aohe o Mele kaikuaana.*
5. Keone has no sisters.	*Aohe o Keone kaikuahine.*
6. I have one canoe.	*Ekahi ou waa.*
7. Mele has no younger sisters.	*Aohe o Mele kaikaina.*

36.1. There are two possible English translations for the following Hawaiian sentence. What are they?

Aohe ou kaikuaana.

36.2. Translate the following sentence into English, and indicate who is speaking, Mele or Keone:

Aohe ou kaikuahine.

36.3. The following English sentences would be difficult to translate directly into Hawaiian. Explain why this is true.

Keone has one brother.
Mele has one younger brother.

Original problem by V. Belikov, published in М.Е. Алексеев, В.И. Беликов, С.М. Евграфова, А.Н. Журинский, Е.В. Муравенко. 1991. Задачи по лингвистике, p. 154. МГУ. Москва.

©2011 English translation and adaptation by Thomas Payne. This problem has been reproduced with the permission of the translator.

(37) Maasai (1/1)**

Maasai is a language spoken by about 800,000 people in East Africa, mostly in Kenya and Tanzania.

As with many languages in East Africa, "tone" is very important in Maasai. The different tones are written as marks above some letters. For example, the letters á, í and ó are all pronounced with high tone. The letters a, i and o are all pronounced with low tone.

There are also some letters in the Maasai alphabet that are not used in English. For example, "ɔ" is a sound like the English wo`rd "awe." "ɛ" is similar to the vowel sound in "let," "ʊ" is like the vowel sound in "hood," and "ɪ" is like the vowel sound in "lit." You don't need to be able to pronounce these words in order to solve the problem. However, you should pay very close attention to the letters and the tone marks.

The following are some sentences in Maasai, and their English translations in random order. Indicate which translation goes with each Maasai sentence by placing the letter of the correct translation in the space provided:

Maasai	English
1. éósh ɔlmʊrraní ɔlásʊráí	_____ A. 'The warrior cuts me.'
2. áadɔ́l ɔlasʊráí	_____ B. 'The warrior cuts the tree for me.'
3. áaósh ɔlmʊrraní	_____ C. 'The warrior cuts it.'
4. ídɔ́l ɔlmʊ́rráni	_____ D. 'I cut the tree for the warrior.'
5. íóshokí ɔlmʊ́rráni ɔlásʊráí	_____ E. 'The warrior hits me.'
6. áduŋokí ɔlmʊ́rráni ɔlchɛtá	_____ F. 'You see the warrior.'
7. ádúŋ ɔlchɛtá	_____ G. 'The warrior hits the snake.'
8. áaduŋokí ɔlmʊrraní ɔlchɛtá	_____ H. 'The snake sees me.'
9. áadúŋ ɔlmʊrraní	_____ I. 'You hit the snake for the warrior.'
10. édúŋ ɔlmʊrraní	_____ J. 'I cut the tree.'

English translations in random order.

Previously published in: Payne, T. 2006. Exploring language structure: A student's guide. Cambridge, pp. 285-286.

© Doris L. Payne, 2011. This problem has been reproduced with the permission of the author.

(38) Getting the Hang of Hangul (1/2)**

Korean is written in a very logical and systematic writing system called Hangul. In the list on the left are 17 Korean words. On the right are listed their pronunciations (and meanings), though not in the same order. (The meanings in parentheses in the table and in the subsequent questions are just for your information, and are not part of the problem.) Note that the transcription has been slightly simplified (made more regular) to help you. The following all represent single sounds: *aw, ch, ng, oo.*

A	탁자	1	awi-too (coat)
B	의자	2	ba-ji (trousers)
C	소파	3	bo-su (bus)
D	찬장	4	chang-moon (window)
E	문	5	chan-jang (cupboard)
F	모자	6	daw-law (road)
G	신발	7	ui-ja (chair)
H	바지	8	gi-cha (train)
I	외투	9	haw-soo (lake)
J	버스	10	ja-jon-go (bicycle)
K	집	11	jib (house)
L	자전거	12	maw-ja (hat)
M	기차	13	moon (door)
N	도로	14	saw-pa (sofa)
O	식당	15	sig-dang (restaurant)
P	창문	16	sin-bal (shoe)
Q	호수	17	tag-ja (table)

© Harold Somers, 2011. This problem has been reproduced with the permission of the author.

(38) Getting the Hang of Hangul (2/2)

38.1. Match the words to their pronunciations.

38.2. Write the following words in Korean:
  A) jag-un (small)
  B) nawng-jang (field)
  C) na-moo (tree)
  D) gaw-mab-sub-ni-da (thank you)

38.3. How are the following words pronounced?
  A) 산 (mountain)
  B) 들반 (field)
  C) 물고기 (fish)
  D) 포탁학니다 (please)

Here are some more Korean words and their pronunciations (again in random order), involving some symbols that you have not seen before.

컴퓨터	bba-lun (fast)
빠른	bi-ssan (expensive)
티셔츠	haw-toil (hotel)
호텔	kaw-ggi-li (elephant)
코끼리	kom-pyoo-to (computer)
비싼	ti-syo-chu (teeshirt)

38.4. How are the following words pronounced?
  a. 가벼운 (light)
  b. 이때 (now)
  c 바꾸다 (to change)
  d. 가운데 (in the middle)
  E. 안녕히게세요 (goodbye)

38.5. Finally, write the following names in Korean:
  A) Han-goog (Korea)
  B) Pyong-yang (capital of North Korea)
  C) Pag Ji Song (a Korean footballer (soccer player): [Pag] is usually written as "Park")
  D) A-il-lion-du (Ireland)

(39) Scrabble® (1/2)**

When Alfred Mosher Butts developed Scrabble® beginning in 1933, he chose the distribution of letters after long and careful consideration. He ultimately decided there should be 100 tiles, with two blanks, and the other 98 divided among the letters as follows:

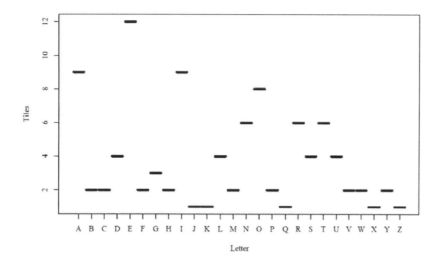

If Butts had simply counted the letters on the front page of *The New York Times*, as is commonly believed, his letter distribution would have been more like this:

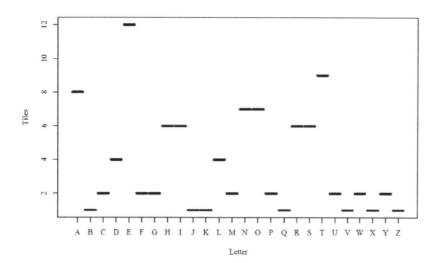

© Roy Tromble, 2011. This problem has been reproduced with the permission of the author.

(39) Scrabble® (2/2)

39.1. Which five letters' counts change the most between the two distributions?

39.2. The Brown Corpus[1] consists of over one million words of text taken from a variety of sources and genres. We will pretend it is a reasonable approximation of the front page of *The New York Times*. The twenty words that occur most frequently in the Brown Corpus are *the, of, and, to, a, in, that, is, was, he, for, it, with, as, his, on, be, at, by,* and *I*, in that order. These twenty words comprise about 31% of the word tokens in the corpus. Here, token refers to an instance of a word in the text.
For which of the letters in your answer to part 1 does this list help explain why the two distributions assign it a different number of tiles?

39.3. The words in part 2 are not equally frequent. Rather, frequency decreases rapidly with rank:, as is se seen in the figure. How does this new information change your answer to part 2?

	Word	Frequency (%)
1.	the	6.8872
2.	of	3.5839
3.	and	2.8401
4.	to	2.5744
5.	a	2.2996
6.	in	2.1010
7.	that	1.0428
8.	is	0.9943
9.	was	0.9661
10.	he	0.9392
11.	for	0.9340
12.	it	0.8623
13.	with	0.7176
14.	as	0.7137
15.	his	0.6886
16.	on	0.6636
17.	be	0.6276
18.	at	0.5293
19.	by	0.5224
20.	I	0.5099

[1] The Brown Corpus (compiled in the 1960s by Henry Kucera and W. Nelson Francis) is a classic corpus (text collection). It contains 500 samples of English-language text, roughly 1,000,000 words, compiled from works published in the United States in 1961.

(40) Walrus (1/1)***

In 1996, a joint session of the orthographical committees from Austria, Germany and Switzerland decided to reform German spelling rules for better consistency. In particular, the letter ß (es-zett) was in some (not all) cases replaced by the letter combination ss. The table below lists some German words in both orthographical variants, as well as the corresponding English words:

German (old orthography)	German (new orthography)	English
Boß	Boss	boss
daß	dass	that
Nuß	Nuss	nut
küß	küss	kiss
mußt	musst	must
Walroß	Walross	walrus
barfuß	barfuß	barefoot
groß	groß	great
Soße	Soße	sauce
Straße	Straße	street
süß	süß	sweet
Auslaß		outlet
Baß		bass
Biß		bit
Floß		float
Fußball		football
Geißhirt		goatherd
grüß		greet
schieß		shoot
Schuß		shot
Schweiß		sweat

40.1. Fill in the omissions in the table, providing the new orthographical versions of the German words.

40.2. Do you think it is easier or harder for the foreigners to read German in the new orthography? Explain your solution.

© Boris Iomdin, 2011. This problem has been reproduced with the permission of the author.

(41) Sentence Endings (1/1)^{***}

A common task that a computer needs to do with text is to identify the words and the sentences. This task is very easy for humans, because we can use our understanding of the meaning of the text to identify the sentences. On the other hand, a but a computer needs to follow very specific rules that do not require any real understanding of the text. An example of a rule is:

IF a period (full stop) is followed by blank spaces plus a capital letter THEN this is a sentence boundary.

Use this rule to find all the sentences in the following text:

> *The Bank of New York ADR Index, which tracks depository receipts traded on major U.S. stock exchanges, gained 1.3% to 183.32 points in recent session. The index lost 4.63 from the beginning of July. American Depositary Receipts are dollar-denominated securities that are traded in the U.S. but represent ownership of shares in a non-U.S. company.*

41.1. Did this rule suffice to find each and every sentence in the above text?

41.2. Give <u>two</u> examples of text that would make the rule fail to split the text into correct sentences. The examples should illustrate different types of failures.

41.3. Write revised rules that would handle any of the problematic examples that you have identified so far.

© Diego Molla-Aliod, 2011. This problem has been reproduced with the permission of the author.

(42) Counting in Etruscan (1/2)***

The Etruscans flourished as a separate people inhabiting parts of northern Italy centered on the region now known as Tuscany for several centuries until the 1st century B.C., when they were effectively absorbed into the expanding Roman Empire. They traded throughout the Mediterranean and acquired their alphabetic writing system from the Greeks, with whom they traded extensively. They left many written texts, which we can easily read, as the Greek alphabet was used; however, their spoken language became extinct, and because Etruscan bears no resemblance to any Indo-European language, we cannot understand the meaning of many words. In fact, Etruscan is only partially deciphered.

Generally, identification of Etruscan numbers remains difficult, but the first six numbers form a group apart. They are found in epitaphs (in which age of the deceased and the number of their children is given) and in the Book of the Mummy, which specifies dates of the periodical religious ceremonies and the size of various offerings.

On a pair of Etruscan dice, known as the Tuscan dice, there are inscribed the following six words, which we give in alphabetic order: *ci, huth, max, sa, thu, zal.* Each of these words corresponds to one of the numbers between 1 and 6 (compare English "one"-1; "two"-2; etc.). You can see how these number words are arranged on the figure below:

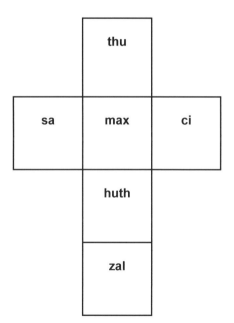

© Luda Kedova and Rachel Nordlinger, 2011. This problem has been reproduced with the permission of the authors.

(42) Counting in Etruscan (2/2)

42.1. Which word corresponds to which number?

At the time of the decipherment, linguists had the following clues:

1) the sum of numbers on the opposite faces of the dice equals 7;

2) *thu*, *ci* and *zal*, in a certain order, represent *1, 2, 3*;

3) *ci*, but not *thu* and *zal*, occurs very frequently in the Book of the Mummy;

4) the following pairs of words were found in epitaphs:
thu clan; thu at; thu mezu; thu vinac; thu thuscu;
ci clenar; zal clenar; ci atr; zal atr; ci mesur; zal mesur; ci vinacr; zal vinacr; ci thuscur;
zal thuscur

5) in several ancient Mediterranean cultures, the number '3' had special, magic-like significance.

Write the correct number under its corresponding written version on the graphic of the dice below:

Now, here's another twist.

It seems that Etruscans enjoyed gambling, as many sets of dice have been found. On one pair, there are inscribed the following six words which we give here in their alphabetic order: *caius, est, i, va, volote, urti*. These were inscribed on the dice rather than the number words found on the Tuscan dice.

Moreover, this choice of words is not random. They are claimed to make up a sentence expressing a popular Etruscan proverb: *volote i va est, caius urti*, meaning 'to a docile horse, the ford is pleasant'.

42.2. Supposing that these words were arranged on the dice to symbolize the numbers written on the Tuscan dice, inscribe each word of this proverb below its corresponding number word in the figure on the previous page.

(43) Tamil I (1/2)****

Below are some words in the Tamil language, transcribed using a system of phonetic symbols developed by American linguists in the 20th century. The symbol ":" following a vowel indicates that it is long; ṭ, ḍ and ṇ are retroflex versions of t, d, n (pronounced with the tongue curled backwards); č sounds like English "ch"; š is like English "sh"; ǰ is like English "j"; ñ is like Spanish ñ in "Español"; ð is like English "th" in "that"; β is like Spanish "v" in "lavar"; ɹ̣ is a retroflex sound like English or Mandarin "r"; γ is like Spanish "g" in "pagar"; ŋ is like English "ng" in "sing"; ḷ is a retroflex version of l; ɨ represents a high central unrounded vowel, like Russian "ы" or Guarani "y".

1.	vi:ḍɨ	house	20.	arivɨ	knowledge
2.	paɹam	fruit	21.	pe:šɨ	speak!
3.	kaβam	phlegm	23.	činna	small
4.	iḍa.ɨ	left	24.	pašikkira.ɨ	is feeling hungry
5.	vaŋgi	bank	25.	toṇḍai	throat
6.	ka:ḍɨ	forest	26.	paṇam	money
7.	ka:ṭṭɨ	show!	27.	naṇḍɨ	crab
8.	añǰɨ	fear!	28.	aŋge:	there
9.	pe:ččɨ	speech	29.	čirippɨ	laughter
10.	čonne:n	I said	30.	aččam	fear
11.	romba	very (colloquial)	31.	viral	finger
12.	maγan	son	32.	namakkɨ	to us
13.	makkaḷ	people	33.	ru:βa:y	rupee
14.	ka:ppa:ṭṭa	to protect	34.	vanda:y	you came
15.	mu.ɨγɨ	back	35.	mo:šam	bad
16.	kuppai	trash	36.	tamiɹ	Tamil
17.	eɹɨ tti	letter	37.	ya:ɹ	harp
18.	eɹɨ .ɨ	write!	38.	ella:m	everything
19.	mu:ñǰi	face (colloquial)	39.	malar	flower

© Anand Natarajan, 2011. This problem has been reproduced with the permission of the author.

(43) Tamil I (2/2)

43.1. If you study the data carefully, you will notice that not all of the sounds appear in all positions in a word. This is called "defective distribution" by linguists. Describe the environments in which each sound in Tamil occurs. You may ignore the consonant "y" for this exercise. If you feel that you don't have enough data to draw a solid conclusion, please mention this.

43.2. In order to describe the sound systems of languages, linguists make use of the notion of the "phoneme." A phoneme is "a contrastive unit in the sound system of a particular language." Give an example In structural linguistics, each phoneme has a series of realizations (actual sounds that are produced by the speaker). Realizations of the same phoneme are called "allophones." Knowing this, how many phonemes are there in Tamil? For each, give their allophones and the environments in which they occur.

(44) The Fall of the Yers (1/1)****

The Slavic languages are a family of languages spoken in Central and Eastern Europe, and form a branch of the Indo-European family. Below are some words in two modern Slavic languages, as well as in Old Church Slavonic — the oldest recorded Slavic language. The symbols ь and ъ are taken from the Cyrillic alphabet and represent unique sounds in Old Church Slavonic (OCS). The symbols oN and ě represent specific OCS vowels (like "on" in French "ton" and like "a" in English "hat," respectively).

OCS	Bulgarian	Russian	English Meaning
dьnь	den	den'	day
gradъ	grad	gorod	city
dъždь	dăžd	dožd'	rain
boNdoN	băda	budu	I am/I will be
igrajoN	igraja	igraju	I play
dьnьsь	dnes	dnes'	today/nowadays
sъnъ	săn	son	sleep
dьni	dni	dni	days
poNtь	păt	put'	path
oNgъlъ	ăgăl	ugol	corner
bělъ	bjal	bel	white
obědъ	objad	obed	lunch
mrazъ	mraz	moroz	frost
nesoN	(do)nesa	nesu	I carry
kostь	kost	kost'	bone

44.1. Fill in the following table:

OCS	Bulgarian	Russian	English Meaning
	bera	beru	I gather/I take
		korol'	king
krъvь			blood
zoNbъ			tooth

44.2. In modern Russian, the symbols ъ and ь are silent, though they affect the pronunciation of the previous consonants. However, linguists think that these letters were not silent in Old Church Slavonic. What kinds of sounds do you think these symbols represented (consonants or vowels)?

The Russian and Bulgarian examples have been transliterated from the Cyrillic alphabet.

© Anand Natarajan, 2011. This problem has been reproduced with the permission of the author.

(45) Eat Your Words! (1/2)***

Arabic is spoken by more than 200 million people as a first language or as a foreign language used in religious practices associated with Islam. There are over 20 main regional spoken varieties, and within these regions, there are further local and social varieties. A more formal variety known as Modern Standard Arabic is spoken by educated people in the Arabic speaking countries.

These words belong to one variety of fast, casual, everyday spoken Arabic:

1.	laHm	*meat*	21.	mishmish	*apricot*
2.	fijli	*a radish*	22.	laymūni	*a lemon*
3.	qāqūni	*a rockmelon*	23.	xyār	*cucumber*
4.	xārūf	*sheep*	24.	baqara	*a cow*
5.	kbīr	*big*	25.	baSli	*an onion*
6.	fraiz	*strawberry*	26.	ka ͨki	*a biscuity cake*
7.	wazz	*goose*	27.	lawz	*almond*
8.	sukkar	*sugar*	28.	laHəm ghazāl	*venison (deer meat)*
9.	ktīr	*much/very*	29.	baqar	*cattle*
10.	mawz	*banana*	30.	filfil	*pepper*
11.	sukkara	*a sugar lump*	31.	laHmi mafrūmi	*ground meat*
12.	qāqūn	*rockmelon*	32.	mishmishi	*an apricot*
13.	zghīr	*little/small*	33.	laymūn	*lemon*
14.	laHmi	*a bit of meat*	34.	shwayyit əxyār	*some cucumber*
15.	xyāra	*a cucumber*	35.	qāqūn əktīr əktīr	*a lot of rockmelon*
16.	wazzi	*a goose*	36.	finjān əzghīr	*a little cup*
17.	fijil	*radish*	37.	lawzi zghīri	*a small almond*
18.	mawzi	*a banana*	38.	al-baSli l-əkbīri	*the big onion*
19.	baSil	*onion*	39.	l-əxyār əl-bārida	*the cold cucumber*
20.	fraizāya	*a strawberry*	40.	Halīb əl-baqara	*milk of the cow*

Pronunciation of unfamiliar letters (not essential knowledge for solving the problem):

j = sound of 'z' in 'a<u>z</u>ure'; i = vowel sound in 's<u>i</u>t'; ī = vowel sound in 's<u>ee</u>d'; u = vowel sound as in 'f<u>u</u>ll'; ū = vowel sound in 'f<u>oo</u>l'; a = vowel in 'c<u>a</u>t'; ā = vowel sound in 'p<u>ea</u>r' ; ə = unstressed vowel as the last vowel in 'hors<u>e</u>s'; ai = as in 'l<u>ie</u>'; D= deeper 'd'; S = a deeper 's'; H: breathy 'h'; x = <u>ch</u> in Scottish 'lo<u>ch</u>'; ͨ = like a growl in the throat; digraph <u>sh</u> = beginning sound of 'she'; digraph <u>gh</u> = the 'r' sound in French '<u>r</u>ouge'. The other letters are like their English equivalents.

© Verna Rieschild, 2011. This problem has been reproduced with the permission of the author.

(45) Eat Your Words! (2/2)

45.1. Write the Arabic equivalent of these English phrases:

English	Arabic Equivalent
a big strawberry	
the big apricot	
some biscuity cake	
a lot of sugar	
a pepper	
beef	

45.2. When does the sound written 'ə' appear in words?

45.3. Why is 'meat' pronounced as laHəm in 28 rather than as laHm in 1, while in 34-36 'ə' is the first sound of the second word in the phrase?

45.4. Why is 'the big (one)' pronounced as l-əkbīri in 38 rather than as al-kbīri following the pattern of al-baSli 'the onion' or as əl-kbīri like əl-bārida in 39?

45.5. Explain the variant forms of 'cucumber' listed below.

'cucumber'	Example No.	Explanation
xyār	23	
xyāra	15	
əxyār	34	
l-əxyār	39	

(46) Noun-Noun Compounds (1/1)***

Noun phrases that consist of two nouns such as "state laws" and "baby chair" (also known as noun-noun compounds) can be categorized based on the preposition that would be used if they were rewritten in the form "NOUN PREPOSITION NOUN". For example, "state laws" = "laws OF the state", "morning prayers" = "prayers IN the morning".

Can you think of other categories of noun-noun compounds that use other prepositions? Give examples of as many categories as you can.

Problem based on Lauer, M. "Designing Statistical Language Learners: Experiments on Noun Compounds". Ph.D. dissertation, Macquarie University, 1995

© Dragomir Radev, 2011. This problem has been reproduced with the permission of the author.

(47) A Killer Puzzle (1/1)*

Here are some English phrases with their Russian translations:

* John killed Mary — Джон убил Мэри
* Mary killed Sam — Мэри убила Сэма
* Sam killed John — Сэм убил Джона

Your task is to translate into Russian the following sentences:

47.1. John killed Sam

47.2. Mary killed John

47.3. Sam killed Mary

© Tanya Khovanova, 2011. This problem has been reproduced with the permission of the author.

(48) It's All Greek to Me (1/2)***

We use many words that have Greek origins, for example: amoral, asymmetric, barometer, chronology, demagogue, dermatology, gynecologist, horoscope, mania, mystic, orthodox, philosophy, photography, polygon, psychology, telegram and telephone. In this puzzle, I assume that you know the meanings of these words. Also, since I am a generous person, I will give you definitions from Answers.com of some additional words derived from Greek. If you do not know these words, you should learn them, as I picked words for this list that gave me at least one million Google results.

- Agoraphobia — an abnormal fear of open or public places.
- Anagram — a word or phrase formed by reordering the letters of another word or phrase, such as satin to stain.
- Alexander — defender of men.
- Amphibian — an animal capable of living both on land and in water.
- Anthropology — the scientific study of the origin, the behavior, and the physical, social, and cultural development of humans.
- Antipathy — a strong feeling of aversion or repugnance.
- Antonym — a word having a meaning opposite to that of another word.
- Bibliophile — a lover of books or a collector of books.
- Dyslexia — a learning disability characterized by problems in reading, spelling, writing, speaking or listening.
- Fibromyalgia — muscle pain.
- Hippodrome — an arena for equestrian shows.
- Misogyny — hatred of women.
- Otorhinolaryngology — the medical specialty concerned with diseases of the ear, nose and throat.
- Polygamy — the condition or practice of having more than one spouse at one time.
- Polyglot — a person having a speaking, reading, or writing knowledge of several languages.
- Tachycardia — a rapid heart rate.
- Telepathy — communication through means other than the senses, as by the exercise of an occult power.
- Toxicology — the study of the nature, effects, and detection of poisons and the treatment of poisoning.
- Pediatrician — A medical practitioner who specializes in medical care of infants, children and adolescents.
- Francophilia — Positive predisposition or interest towards the government, culture, history and people of France.

48.1. In the list below, I picked very rare English words with Greek origins. You can derive the meanings of these words without looking in a dictionary, just by using your knowledge of the Greek words above.

- Barology
- Bibliophobia
- Cardialgia
- Dromomania
- Gynophilia

© Tanya Khovanova, 2011. This problem has been reproduced with the permission of the author.

(48) It's All Greek to Me (2/2)

- Misandry
- Misanthropy
- Misogamy
- Monandry
- Monoglottism
- Mystagogue
- Pedagogue
- Philanthropism

48.2. Here are some other words. You do not have enough information in this text to derive their definitions, but you might be able to use your erudition to guess the meaning.

- Antinomy
- Apatheist
- Axiology
- Dactyloscopy
- Enneagon
- Oology
- Paraskevidekatriaphobia
- Philadelphia
- Phytology
- Triskaidekaphobia

(49) Zoque (1/2)***

Zoque is a language from southern central Mexico. There are several dialects of Zoque which are spoken by over 30,000 indigenous Mexicans. The Zoque language is a member of the larger Mixe-Zoque group of languages.

Zoque words can be very complex, incorporating parts which mark plural and also parts expressing meanings which in English are expressed by separate words (such as prepositions, e.g., *on, for...*). An example of an English complex word is *un-manag(e)-abil-ity*.

Study these Zoque words:
Note: ə represents the vowel sound of English 'e' in *open*; ʔ represents a glottal stop, which is the sound we get in the middle of the expression of disagreement *nuh-uh*; ŋ is the consonant sound represented by 'ng', as in *sing*; š is the sound written 'sh' in *she*.

1.	pən	*man*	11.	yomo	*woman*
2.	pəntaʔm	*men*	12.	yomohiʔŋ	*with a woman*
3.	pənkəsi	*on a man*	13.	yomotih	*just a woman*
4.	pənkotoya	*for a man*	14.	yomoʔune	*girl*
5.	pənhiʔŋ	*with a man*	15.	kahši	*hen*
6.	pənkəsitaʔm	*on men*	16.	kahšiʔune	*chick*
7.	pənkəsišeh	*as on a man*	17.	maŋu teʔ pən	*The man went*
8.	pənšeh	*manlike*	18.	maŋpa teʔ pən	*The man goes.*
9.	pənšehtaʔm	*like men*	19.	maŋkeʔtpa teʔ yomo	*The woman also goes.*
10.	teʔ pən	*the man*	20.	minpa teʔ ʔune	*The child comes.*

49.1. List all of the meaningful parts of these Zoque words and write their English equivalent beside it. Two examples are done for you.

Zoque	English	Zoque	English
pən	*man*	hiʔŋ	*with*

© Mary Laughren, 2011. This problem has been reproduced with the permission of the author.

(49) Zoque (2/2)

49.2. Translate into Zoque:

English	Zoque
The child came	
The girl also went	
with children	
for women	

49.3. Translate into English:

Zoque	English
maŋutih teʔ yomoʔune	
yomotihtaʔm	

Data from: Nida, E. (1974) Morphology: The Descriptive Analysis of Words (second edition). Ann Arbor, Mich.: The University of Michigan Press.

(50) Pitjantjatjara (1/2)***

Pitjantjatjara is one of the Western Desert languages spoken by about 2,000 Australian Aboriginal people living in the northern part of South Australia and the southwest part of the Northern Territory.

Here are some examples of English words which have been incorporated into Pitjantjatjara. Some of them are pronounced in a similar way to their English counterparts, whereas others are pronounced in ways that are quite different.

English	Pitjantjatjara	English	Pitjantjatjara
teacher	tiitja	*John*	Tjaana
paper	piipa	*school*	kuula
shovel	tjapila	*bus*	paatja
room	ruuma	*tent*	tiinta
crowbar	kurupa	*flour*	palawa
ration	ratjina	*bucket*	pakata
rabbit	rapita	*drunk (inebriated)*	tarangka

Note: The vowel 'a' is pronounced like the vowel in *but* or *us* while 'aa' is a 'long a' pronounced more like the vowel written 'a' in *father*. The vowel written 'i' is pronounced like the vowel in *bit*, while *ii* is 'long i', which is more like the vowel sound in *bee* or *seed*. The vowel *u* is like the vowel in *put*, while the 'long u', written as *uu*, is more like the vowel sound in *school* or *pool*. The long vowels, *ii, uu, aa*, in the Pijantjatjara words tend to be longer than in the corresponding English word. The letters *tj* represent a sound similar to English *ch* in *chin*, but a little closer to *t*, especially if followed by the vowel *a*. You will notice that English 's' changes into the Pitjantjatjara *tj* sound.

By comparing the English and Pitjantjatjara pairs of words, we can learn quite a bit about the vowel and consonant sounds of Pitjantjatjara, and also about the way in which these sounds may or may not pattern to form words. We can also see that certain rules or processes are applied in converting English words into Pitjantjatjara ones.

Hint: To answer the questions below, it is important to think about how the English words *sound* and not just how they are written.

50.1. Under what condition must the initial vowel in these Pitjantjatjara words be a long vowel (written *aa*, *uu*, or *ii*)?

50.2. All these Pitjantjatjara words borrowed from English end in 'a'. Does this word final vowel have a single source or origin? Explain the reasoning behind your answer.

© Mary Laughren, 2011. This problem has been reproduced with the permission of the author.

(50) Pitjantjatjara (2/2)

50.3. **a.** Which sequences of consonant sounds are not permitted in the Pitjantjatjara words?
b. Which examples illustrate this?
c. How have the Pitjantjatjara speakers changed the sequence of sounds to avoid an 'illegal' consonant sequence inherited from the English borrowing?

50.4. **a.** Which English sounds correspond to the Pitjantjatjara sound written 'p'?
b. What do the English sounds you have listed in answering Question 4a have in common? (HINT: Say them silently to yourself and note which part of your mouth moves in order to pronounce these sounds.)

50.5. **a.** If English *blood* were borrowed into Pitjantjatjara, how would the Pitjantjatjara word be written?
b. Set out your reasoning for the form you have written for *blood*.

Data from: Goddard, Cliff. 1992. Pitjantjatjara/Yankunytjatjara to English Dictionary (Second Edition). Alice Springs: Institute for Aboriginal Development Press.

(51) String Transformers (1/1)***

This problem is about rules that turn things into other things. You start with a sequence (or 'string') of characters. If your string contains a character that appears on the left side of the arrow in a rule, you can turn that character into whatever is on the right side of the arrow in that rule. You can apply different rules to your string over and over again until no more moves are possible. You're not allowed to twiddle the order of the characters in your string.

Here are the rules:

$S \rightarrow AB$
$A \rightarrow ab$
$A \rightarrow aAb$
$B \rightarrow bcd$
$B \rightarrow bBc$

51.1. If you start with 'S', which of these strings is it possible to end up with using these rules?

1. abcd
2. abbcd
3. aabbbcd
4. aaabbbcd
5. abbbbcdcc
6. aabbccdcc
7. aabbbbcdc
8. aaabbbbcd
9. aaabbbbcdc
10. aabbbbbcdcc
11. aaabbbbbbcdcc

51.2. Here is a string that can not be generated by these rules: **bbbbcdccc**. Can you add a rule to all the others so that this string can be generated?

© Daniel Midgley, 2011. This problem has been reproduced with the permission of the author.

(52) Nen (1/2)***

Nen is a Papuan language with around 300 speakers spoken in just one village – Bimadeben – in the Trans-Fly region just across the Torres Strait from Australia. This region is geographically very similar to Australia, with eucalypts, melaleucas, kangaroos, bandicoots and taipans, and many Nen people look like Aboriginal people, though the language does not appear to be related to Australian languages. Nick Evans recently began field-work on this language. There are about 30 undescribed languages in the Trans-Fly region belonging to 8 unrelated families.

Consider the examples, then answer the questions on the next page:

1	I work	yánd nogiabtan
2	you (one person) work	bám nogiabte
3	he or she works	bä nogiabte
4	I talk	yánd nowabtan
5	I return	yánd nánanḡtan
6	you (one person) return	bám nánanḡte
7	he or she talks	bä nowabte
8	we (three or more) work	yánd nogiabtam
9	we (three or more) return	yánd nánanḡtam
10	you (three or more) work	bám nogiabtat
11	you (three or more) return	bám nánanḡtat
12	they (three or more) talk	bä nowabtat
13	they (three or more) work	bä nogiabtat
14	we two work	yánd nogiabám
15	you two return	bám nnanḡt
16	they two talk	bä nowabát
17	they two return	bä nnanḡát
18	we two talk	yánd nowabám

a is a long *ah* as in *ta* for 'thank you', *ä* is like its German value (close to *a* in English cat). Other vowels have the values they would in Italian or Indonesian. ḡ is a simultaneously articulated g and b with a w-like release. These pronunciations, however, are not relevant to the questions asked in this problem.

© Nick Evans, 2011. This problem has been reproduced with the permission of the author.

(52) Nen (2/2)

52.1. How would you say the following:

you (one person) talk _____

he or she returns _____

they (three or more) return _____

we (three or more) talk _____

you two work _____

52.2. What words and/or parts of words do you need in order to express the English words

a 'I'
b 'they (more than two)'

52.3. What would be the best translation for the words

a yánd
b bä

52.4. How would you best define the meaning of the *t* found in *nogiabtan* in example 1 and in examples 2-13 ?

52.5. How do you express the idea that two people are carrying out the action?

52.6. You hear a new phrase *yánd neretan* 'I listen'. Hearing that, how do you think you would say 'they (three or more) listen'?

(53) Enga (1/3)****

Enga is a language spoken by over 150,000 people in the Enga area in the highlands of Papua New Guinea.

Enga verbs always incorporate a sound or sequence of sounds indicating whether it is the speaker or addressee, or another person (or some combination of these), who is being referred to by the *subject* word or phrase in the sentence (typically referring to the person doing the action, or who is in the state denoted by the verb). A small number of 'give' verbs also incorporate information about who something is being given to.

Consider these sentences, which are about the gift of a pig. These sentences contain information about both the 'pig-giver' and the 'pig-receiver'. Pigs play a very important role in the economic and social life of Enga people.

1.	Namba-mé	émba	mená méndé	dílio.	*I am giving you a pig.*
	I-agent	you	pig a	give	
2.	Émba-me	nambá	mená méndé	dilíno.	*You are giving me a pig.*
	you-agent	me	pig a	give	
3.	Baa-mé	nambá	mená méndé	diliámo.	*He is giving me a pig.*
	he-agent	me/you	pig a	give	
4.	Baa-mé	émba	mená méndé	diliámo.	*He is giving you a pig.*
	he-agent	you	pig a	give	
5.	Namba-mé	baá	mená méndé	maílio.	*I am giving him a pig.*
	I-agent	him	pig a	give	
6.	Émba-me	baá	mená méndé	mailíno.	*You are giving him a pig.*
	you-agent	him	pig a	give	
7.	Baa-mé	baá	mená méndé	mailiámo.	*He is giving him a pig.*
	he-agent	him	pig a	give	
8.	Baa-mé	baá	mená méndé	maipiámo.	*He gave him a pig.*
	he-agent	him	pig a	gave	
9.	Baa-mé	baá	mená méndé	maitámo	*He will give him a pig.*
	he-agent	him	pig a	will_give	

© Mary Laughren, 2011. This problem has been reproduced with the permission of the author.

(53) Enga (2/3)

Part I.

Focusing on the forms of the verb (= last word in each sentence):

53.1. Which part of the <u>verb</u> indicates the *giver*? Write the Enga forms which correspond to the English word in the indicated sentences.

Sentence	English	Enga
1 & 5	I	
2 & 6	you	
3,4, 7, 8, 9	he	

53.2. Which part of the <u>verb</u> indicates the *receiver*? Write the Enga forms which correspond to the English word in the indicated sentences.

Sentence	English	Enga
1 & 4	you	
2 & 3	me	
5-9	him	

53.3. (a) Circle the part of the following three verbs that expresses the **time** of the 'giving' event relative to the time at which the sentence is uttered, and (b) indicate whether it marks *present, past* or *future* by writing this under the matching verb. (The number indicates the sentence the verb is taken from.)

    7. *mailiámo*   8. *maipiámo*   9. *maitámo*

53.4. Circle the part of the verb that expresses the idea of *giving* in the following verbs taken from the sentences indicated by the number.

    1. *dílio*   2. *dilino*   5. *mailíno*   9. *maitámo*

(53) Enga (3/3)

Part 2.

Although *li* is written in the verbs in 1-7 whether it is followed by a consonant or a vowel, when it is followed by a vowel (a, e, i, o, u), the 'i' is not pronounced as a full 'i' sound as in English *lit* (or *lee*), so that *dílio* in sentence 1 is not pronounced as *di-li-o* (or *dee-lee-o*), but rather it is pronounced *di-lyo* (*ly* is like in English *million* which is pronounced as two syllables *mil-yon* and <u>not</u> as three syllables: *mi-li-on* or *mi-lee-on*).

Each Enga verb has one accented syllable marked by an acute accent symbol (´) over the accented vowel.

53.5. Is it possible to predict which syllable of each verb will receive the accent? Explain the reasons for your answer, showing how your explanation can account for the accent placement on the verb in sentences 1, 2, 3 and 5.

53.6. Comparing the placement of the accent on the first word of each sentence and the accent on the pronoun, which is the second word, can you account for the variable placement of the accent on the first word: either on the first syllable or the final syllable?

Data from Lang, Adrianne (1975) The semantics of classificatory verbs in Enga (and other Papua New Guinea languages). Pacific Linguistics B-39. Canberra: ANU.

(54) News Tag (1/1)****

Our news aggregator site attempts to automatically tag articles according to their category. At least, that's what it tries to do. Usually, it works fine, but sometimes it goes hilariously wrong. Here are some headlines that the algorithm mis-categorized. What are the missing words? What is the overall cause for the errors?

- More 60-year olds plan to _____ early. → **Cars**

- Man sues _____ for pulling wrong tooth. → **Cars**

- Player sustains major _____ on field. → **Law**

- Later this week Nicaragua is expected to _____ its constitution. → **Zoology**

- The author used _____ in presenting the protagonist's bad experiences. → **Chemistry**

- The engineers at Boeing are experts in the dynamics of _____. → **Medicine**

- This agreement _____ the incident, so it will remain in effect. → **Zoology**

Can you come up with more such examples ?

© Dragomir Radev, 2011. This problem has been reproduced with the permission of the author.

(55) Hebrew (1/2)****

The Hebrew Language is a member of the Semitic branch of the Afro-Asiatic language family. It has about seven million speakers and is one of the two official languages of Israel (along with Arabic). In this problem, 'x' represents [x], the "ch" sounds in the words "Bach" and "loch". 'c' represents [ts], the "ts" sounds in the words "cats" and "rats". A single quote (') represents [ʔ], a glottal stop, like the sound in the middle of the word "uh-oh". An acute accent (e.g., á) represents stress.

Below are some sentences in the Hebrew language, along with their translations in English (in order). Use these to answer the questions below, making sure to show your work

1.	Hamazleg nafal mehayad shelo kshera'a oti.	*The fork fell from his hand when he saw me.*
2.	Ra'íti shoxet mexaded et hasakin shelo.	*I saw a slaughterer sharpening his knife.*
3.	Shaxáteti et hatarnególet baxuc.	*I will slaughtered the chicken outside.*
4.	Im timkor máshehu, ekne oto.	*If you sell something, I will buy it.*
5.	Káxa shoxatim para.	*This is how one slaughters a cow.*
6.	Beshuk hu ra'a anashim moxrim dvarim.	*In a market he saw people selling things.*
7.	Ha'isha ro'a et hayalda mesaxéket verokédet mibá'ad lexalon.	*The woman sees the girl playing and dancing through a window.*
8.	Maxárti et kol hazahav sheli, kaníti séfer al rikud, verakádeti baxuc	*I sold all my gold, bought a book on dancing, and danced outside.*
9.	Lo sixáktiksheDavid xazar mehakinus.	*I didn't play when David returned from the conference.*
10.	Hem tamid zoxrim la'asot et hashi'urim.	*They always remember to do the homework.*
11.	Emkor et haxamor lexa bezol.	*I will sell the donkey to you at a low price.*
12.	Anashim boxrim et hanasi.	*People elect the president.*

Questions 1 and 2 ask about certain sound changes that have occurred in the Hebrew language. Explain your reasoning in your answers to both.

55.1. The sound "x" was originally pronounced as "k" in some words in an older stage of Hebrew. Give an example of such a word.

55.2. A consonant cluster is a group of adjacent consonants, such as the cluster "sp" in the word "spoon." Certain consonant clusters existed in older Hebrew that are no longer consonant clusters in Modern Hebrew. Give five such clusters.

© Morris Alper, 2011. This problem has been reproduced with the permission of the author.

(55) Hebrew (2/2)

55.3. Translate the following sentences into English:

    A. Tir'e anashim mesaxakim verokdim baxuc.
    B. Hasakin tamid nofel al hayad shelo.
    C. Xidádeti oto vehashoxet kana oto.

55.4. Translate the following sentences into Hebrew:

    A. I will remember to do my homework.
    B. You will not buy gold at a low price.
    C. The woman slaughters the donkey outside.

(56) Japanese Kanazukai (1/2)***

Kanazukai refers to any system for spelling the Japanese language using Kana, the native syllabic scripts. Kyuukanazukai was the system used before World War II, which reflected the pronunciation of the Heian Period (794-1185). After the war, Japan adopted the Shinkanazukai system, which was designed to reflect modern pronunciation. This problem uses a variation of Hepburn Romanization.

Below is a chart of Japanese words, written using the historical and modern systems. Use these to answer the questions below, making sure to show your work.

Kyuukanazukai	Shinkanazukai	English
Wefu	You	To get seasick/drunk
Kiuri	Kyuuri	Cucumber
Deseu	Deshou	Probably is
Tafutoi	Toutoi	Exalted
Wobasan	Obasan	Aunt
Kowe	Koe	Voice
Kaha	Kawa	River
Jifuji	Juuji	10 o'clock
Te	Te	Hand
Kaheru	Kaeru	To return
Takubokuteu	Takubokuchou	Woodpecker
Ahimasu	Aimasu	To meet
Wiru	Iru	Is/exists
Washitsu	Washitsu	Japanese-style room

© Morris Alper, 2011. This problem has been reproduced with the permission of the author.

(56) Japanese Kanazukai (2/2)

56.1. Fill in the table below:

Kyuukanazakai	Shinkanazukai	English
Keushitsu		Classroom
Wotoko		Male
Tefu		Butterfly
Ikau		Let's go
Kefu		Today
Kifudai		To pass an exam
Ahare		Sorrow

56.2. What sound changes have occurred since the Heian period? Which can you place in chronological order? (Try to answer using as few and as simple steps as possible.)

Volume I
Solutions

D. Radev (ed.), *Puzzles in Logic, Languages and Computation: The Red Book*, Recreational Linguistics 1,
DOI 10.1007/978-3-642-34378-0_2, © Springer-Verlag Berlin Heidelberg 2013

(1) We Are All Molistic in a Way (1/1)

None of the adjectives are real English words. There are two classes of adjectives: "bad" and "good". We will refer to this property of adjectives as "polarity".

Each sentence links two or more adjectives as follows: "X and Y" indicates that X and Y have the same polarity. "X but Y" means that they have opposite polarities. Furthermore, "X and not Y" indicates opposite polarities, "even though X, Y" also indicates opposite polarities, while "not only X but also Y" associates adjectives of the same polarity. One can use a graph (see picture below) to keep track of these constraints.

The sentence about Diane shows that "strungy" and "struffy" are positive (desirable) qualities. By identifying other occurrences of the same words in other sentences, one can label each adjective as either positive or negative.

There are seven positive adjectives:

strungy
struffy
cloovy
frumsy
danty
cluvious
brastic

and five negative adjectives:

weasy
blitty
sloshful
slatty
molistic

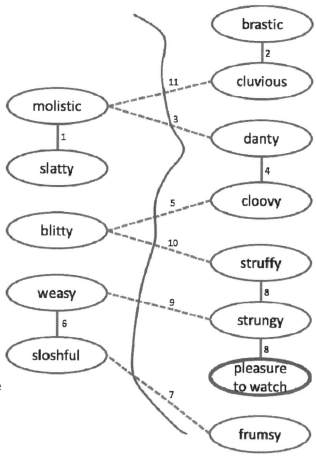

Dashed lines link adjectives that have opposite polarities whereas solid lines are used to link items with the same polarity. The small numbers correspond to the sentence number with the relevant evidence. The curvy line in the middle is used to "cut" all negative links and keep all positive links. The oval around "pleasure to watch" is the only one whose polarity is known. It can be used to label all other ovals.

1.1. Only sentence **c.** connects adjectives of the right polarities.

1.2. Only answer **d.** ("frumsy") is on the positive list above.

(2) Pooh's Encyclopedia (1/1)

The retrieval is based on simple keyword matching: the search engine compares the word roots in a given query with those in article titles, and identifies the titles that have at least two word roots in common with the query. Note that when matching irregular verbs, it determines their roots based on their present tense (e.g. "write" for "wrote"). The matches for the questions by Pooh and his friends are as follows; the matching words are marked by capital letters.

Winnie-the-Pooh:

> Query: Where should a BEAR STOCK his jars of honey?
> Match: Lost tales of "Bulls vs. BEARS" STOCK trading

> Query: How much honey should a BEAR store for the WINTER?
> Match: WINTER hibernation of BEARS and rodents

Eeyore:

> Query: Where should I LOOK for my LOST tail?
> Match: Ways to LOOK for LOST things

> Query: Which ANIMALS SLEEP during the winter?
> Match: Effects of honey on the SLEEP quality of humans and ANIMALS

Christopher Robin:

> Query: What is the shortest WAY from my place to the HOUSE of Winnie-the-Pooh?
> Match: WAYS to store food in the HOUSE

> Query: Who wrote the BOOKS about Pooh BEAR?
> Match: BOOKS about care and feeding of BEARS

(3) A Donkey in Every House (1/2)

3.1. The alignments are as follows:

Greek Sentence	English Sentence
A	5
B	6
C	2
D	3
E	1
F	8
G	7
H	4

In order to align the Ancient Greek sentences with the English sentences, you have figured out the content words (master, son, donkey, house, and slave) and the singulars and plurals. In order to get started, you need an anchor. Once you have an anchor, you can figure out the rest by logic and process of elimination.

Various anchors are possible. Three are described here.

1. Notice that four English sentences contain the word "master" or "masters" and that four Greek sentences contain words that start with "cyr". No other word occurs four times. Therefore, "master" would be "cyr".

2. Count singulars and plurals. For example, in five English sentences, the second noun is plural, and five Greek sentences have the word "ton".

3. Although you can do this problem without recognizing any words, you might have recognized a few. For example, "adelphoi" looks like "Philadelphia", the city of brotherly love. If you know that "phil" means "love", as in "bibliophile" (book lover), then you would know that "adelphoi" means brother. You might also notice that "emporoi" reminds you of the word "emporium", which is a market place.

3.2.
the houses of the merchants	hoi tōn emporōn oicoi
the donkeys of the slave	hoi tu dulu onoi

(3) A Donkey in Every House (2/2)

Vocabulary:

hyi	son
dul	slave
cyri	master
oic	house
on	donkey
adelph	brother
empor	merchant

Order of words:
Each sentence starts with two articles, which are followed by two nouns. The first article starts with "h". The second article starts with "t". The first noun is the owner, and the second noun is the thing that is owned.

Number (singular and plural):
For the owner (first noun in Greek; second noun in English): "ōn" is plural and "u" is singular.
For the owned (second noun in Greek; first noun in English): "oi" is plural and "os" is singular.

Matching of articles and nouns:
The first article has an ending that matches the owned noun: "ho" is singular and "hoi" is plural.

Matching of articles and nouns:
The first article has an ending that matches the owned noun: "ho" is singular and "hoi" is plural.

Examples:
ho .... dulos
the ... slave (singular)

hoi ... cyroi
the ... masters (plural)

The second article matches the owner: "tu" is singular and "tōn" is plural.

Examples:
tu cyriu
the master (singular)

tōn hyiōn
the sons (plural)

96

(4) Hmong (1/1)

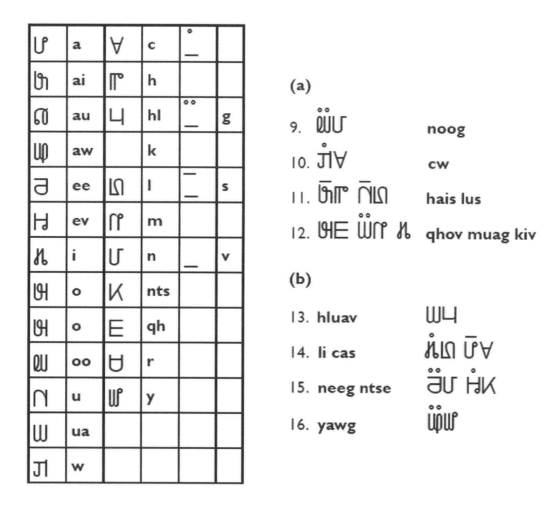

ሆ	a	∀	c	˚_	
ᚦ	ai	ᚦ	h		
ᚷ	au	ᚄ	hl	˚˚_	g
ᚕ	aw		k		
ᚨ	ee	ᚲ	l	‾_	s
ᚺ	ev	ᚱ	m		
ᚼ	i	ᚢ	n	_	v
ᚷ	o	K	nts		
ᚷ	o	E	qh		
ᚳ	oo	ᚦ	r		
∩	u	ᚹ	y		
ᚹ	ua				
ᚾ	w				

(a)

9. Ůᛁᚢ   noog

10. ᛃI∀   cw

11. ᚦᚱ ᚾᚳ   hais lus

12. ᚷᛖ Ůᚱ ᚼ   qhov muag kiv

(b)

13. hluav   ᚹᚻ

14. li cas   ᚼᚳ ᚢ∀

15. neeg ntse   ᚨᚢ ᚺK

16. yawg   Ůᚹᚹ

The syllables are written from right to left, as in the Roman script; however, within a syllable the vowel is written first, then the consonant. (This is so because Shong Lue Yang felt that the vowel was the more prominent sound, and the consonant a mere modification.) There is a letter for each vowel, and also letters for all consonants except **k**, which is pronounced by default if no consonant is indicated. The tone is indicated as a superscript mark above the vowel; both Shong Lue Yang's script and the missionaries' leave one of the four tones unmarked, but their choices are different.

(5) Better Sorry than Shunk (1/1)

5.1.   Here are some options.

She used to _shink_ possums.
Now she _shinks_ groundhogs for a living.
When she was in Eugene, she _shank_ thirty-three possums in one day.
Then she took us possum-_shinking_ in the Cascades.

This is the most likely set of forms for this verb, because of the relatively large number of real verbs that work this way in English, e.g., *drink, drinks, drank, drinking, drunk*; *shrink, shrinks, shrank, shrinking, shrunk*; *sing, sings, sang, singing, sung*; *sink, sinks, sank, sinking, sunk*, etc. These can serve as analogical models for new verb forms, e.g., children sometimes say things like "I brang my new toy" on this analogy.

5.2.   There are many, potentially an infinite number of, possible solutions to E1. The second most likely solutions are based on the analogy of other real verbs that have a "short u" sound in the form that follows "had", e.g.,

shank, shanks, shunk, shanking, shunk based on *hang, hangs, hung, hanging, hung* (the alternate conjugations of this verb take "hanged" after "have," e.g., "They have already hanged the murderer.").

shink, shinks, shunk, shinking, shunk based on *dig, digs, dug, digging, dug.*

shunk, shunks, shank, shunking, shunk based on *run, runs, ran, running, run.* (This is less likely because there is only one verb in English that acts this way).

Much less likely:
shunk, shunks, shunk, shunking, shunk base on *cut, cuts, cut, cutting, cut.* (This is less likely because this class of real verbs in English all end in *t* or *d*, not *k* or *g*.

Even less likely:
There may be any number of random forms of this verb, say *yerkle, blumbles, jambolick, borging, shunk.* Since this is a nonsense verb, and some verbs (like "to be" and "to go") are very irregular in English, it is impossible to limit the possible forms it could take. However, this solution is extremely unlikely, since in fact no verbs in English are totally random in their patterns, and those that are nearly so (like "to be" and "to go") are verbs that are used very often. Presumably "to shink/shunk" would not be such a common verb.

(6) The Lost Tram (1/2)

6.1. The deviations in each text fragment are marked in bold and corrected:

(1)

The **tram** (→**train**) makes no stops; you sit **clown** (→**down**) and are served; there are no further intrusions, no **late-corners** (→**late-comers**), no one hurrying to get off. The businessmen leaf through their financial reports, the lady with the hatbox is alone with her novel and her sirloin. Diners reading: you never see that on a plane. When the coast approaches **arid** (→**and**) dinner is over, everyone retires to his compartment to **he** (→**be**) transferred to the boat in peace, horizontally. *(Sunrise With Seamonsters, by Paul Theroux)*

(2)

Usually, Howie could legitimately claim to have no **dear** (→**fear**) of any man or beast… Howie knew in his heart that it was **he** (→**the**) vulnerable positions he ended up in that scared him. He was used to operating from a position of strength, either real or projected. Now here he was, injured and alone, standing with **and** (→**an**) empty handgun in an open **filed** (→**field**), while **hid** (→**his**) opponent or opponents **fried** (→**fired**) their weapon from behind solid cover. *(Rough Justice, by Mark Johnstone)*

(3)

Two other factors **effect** (→**affect**) the body's temperature regulation: age and acclimatization. As we grow older, we **loose** (→**lose**) our ability to quickly regulate temperature… Very small children are also subject to heat disorders. **There** (→**Their**) small size allows them to take on heat much faster **then** (→**than**) adults. They also cannot indicate their thirst, **accept** (→**except**) through irritability. They are completely dependent upon adults to make certain they get enough fluids. *(Doctor in the House: Your Best Guide to Effective Medical Self-Care, by John Harbert)*

6.2. In the first text fragment, graphically similar letters or letter combinations are mixed up: **m→in, m→rn, ri→n, cl→d, h→b.** This might have occurred if the text (probably messily printed or handwritten) had been interpreted by a computer (using an OCR, optical character recognition software) or (less probably) by a human who hadn't been paying attention to what he had been reading.

In the second text fragment, letters are skipped, added, rearranged or replaced by other letters (in the latter case, the pairs of letters corresponded to neighboring keys on a standard QWERTY keyboard: **d→f, d→s**). This most probably occurred when someone was typing too fast.

In the third text fragment, there are several lexical errors, when words with identical or very similar pronunciation are mixed up. This might have occurred if the person who had copied the text was quite bad at spelling, or maybe if the text was analyzed by a speech recognition system.

(6) The Lost Tram (2/2)

6.3. Common spellchecking programs would not be of much help, since all wrong words are still English words (maybe the texts had already been through a spellcheck). To find at least a partial solution to fixing such deviations, one might create huge lists containing (1) common OCR mistakes (pairs of graphically similar words), (2) common misprints, and (3) commonly confused words. Some such lists already exist. Then, one could trace some (probably not all) mistakes using two alternative approaches. First, one could parse the texts using a natural language processing system, which might find some grammatical (mostly syntactical) mistakes. Constructing such systems is a very topical issue in modern computational linguistics, and a very complicated task. Second, one could verify all suspicious word combinations by searching them in a large text corpus, database, or simply in the web, and comparing the number of hits to that of the alternative combination found in the lists. For example, a Google search yields some 8,690,000 results for **sit down**, and only 252 results for **sit clown** (probably most of them containing the same OCR error). This approach, however, only works for frequent word combinations and could accidentally result in wrong corrections for some rare, but not erroneous combinations. Therefore, the program should be an interactive one, marking potential mistakes and offering the user a variety of ways to correct them, but not attempting to correct them automatically.

(7) Rewrite me Badd (1/1)

Proto-Tangkhulic form:	-ru ("bone")	-khuk ("knee")	-ko ("nine")
Rule 1: K-Deletion			
Intermediate form 1:	-ru	-khu?	-ko
Rule 2: K-Insertion			
Intermediate form 2:	-ruk	-khu?	-ko
Rule 3: V-Raising			
Huishu form:	**-ruk**	**-khu?**	**-ku**

(8) This Problem is Pretty // Easy (1/2)

There are two things going on in the example sentences that are given in the problem statement. One is a change in meaning that is potentially disastrous:

1. You don't need to come // early.
2. Take the turkey out at five // to four.
3. I got canned // peaches.

The second is a confusion factor caused by a change in sentence structure:

4. All Americans need to buy a house // is a lot of money.
6. Fat people eat // accumulates in their bodies.

8.1. Your example sentences need to meet some minimal criteria:

1. The part before // should be a complete sentence.
2. The full sentence has a different meaning than the part before //.
2a. The part before // should not already be ambiguous.

8.2. You were asked to rank two sentences that you made up along with sentences 4, 5, and 6.

4. All Americans need to buy a house // is a lot of money.
5. Melanie is pretty // busy.
6. Fat people eat // accumulates in their bodies.

If you take the confusion factor into account, 4 is the most confusing, followed by 6, and then 5.

8.3. All garden path sentences (a linguistic term for sentences that, when read left to right, seem to change their meaning part of the way through them) are either surprising or confusing, but what makes some harder than others? Looking at sentences 1-6, you might observe a number of things.

1. Change in part of speech: "fat" changes from an adjective in "fat people eat" to a noun in "fat accumulates in their bodies".

2. Change in structure: When you hear "fat people eat", you think that "eat" is the main verb of the sentence. When you hear "accumulates in their bodies", you realize that "people eat" modifies "fat" and that the main verb of the sentence is "accumulates".

(8) This Problem is Pretty // Easy (2/2)

3. Missing words: 4 and 6 would become more clear if the word "that" were inserted:

All that Americans need to buy a house is a lot of money.
Fat that people eat accumulates in their bodies.

4. Intonation: 4 and 6 could be clarified with intonation.

5. Number of words before //: 6 has more words before // than 4 does.

6. Plausibility of the part before //: If you hear a complete and plausible sentence before //, you are less likely to expect more words. "All Americans need to buy a house" is a very plausible thing to say and is a complete sentence. "Fat people eat" is a generic statement, and you might be want to hear more, so you might be expecting more words.

7. Words change meaning: "canned" can mean "fired" or "stored in a can".

8. Level of surprise: "I got canned" meaning "I was fired" could be a very surprising thing to say, and it is quite different from talking about groceries such as "canned peaches".

(9) Of Monkeys and Children (1/1)

9.1.

Ape ratš mï mɛtš.	'The good man works a lot.'
Kukr̃ɛ ratš kokoi punui.	'The bad monkey eats a lot.'
Ape piŋetš mï.	'The man works a long time.'

9.2.

Ape piŋetš kra ratš.	'The big child works a long time.'
Kukr̃ɛ ratš kokoi piŋetš.	'The old monkey eats a lot.'

9.3. ratš means "large in physical size or quantity"; it is interpreted as "big" when following a word like "monkey" or "child," and as "a lot" when following the action word.

mɛtš means "good" or "well"; it is interpreted as "good" when following a word like "man," and as "well" when following the action word.

piŋetš means "long time"; it is interpreted as "old" when following a word like "man" or "monkey," and as "a long time" when following the action word.

(10) Springing up Baby (1/1)

When a word has multiple uses, we distinguish these uses by context. When going from English to Hindi, we can determine the intended meaning of "spring" from the rest of the English sentence. When going from Hindi to English, we look for other parts of the string that the "yesterday" examples have in common with each other, but not with the "tomorrow" examples.

10.1. कूद and वसन्त are the translations of "spring."

10.2. वसन्त is the translation of "spring" in the sentence "we always look forward to the spring holidays."

10.3. In the sentence "we always look forward to the spring holidays," the word "spring" is used in the "season" sense rather than the "jump" sense. In the provided examples, when "spring" is used in the "season" sense, the word वसन्त appears in the Hindi translation. Note that the "jump" sense of "spring" corresponds to a verb in Hindi, and it appears in different tenses, which have different endings in Hindi. Its forms include कूदने, कूद, and कूदकर ; the common root is कूद .

10.4. The two translations of कल are "yesterday" and "tomorrow."

10.5. "Yesterday" is the translation of कल in the sentence

अनामिका यहाँ कल आयी थी ।

10.6. The word थी from this sentence also appears in both sentences where कल means "yesterday," and in none of the sentences where कल means "tomorrow." Since थी resolves कल to "yesterday," we conclude that it places the described event in the past.

(11) Reach for the Top (1/1)

11.1.

ꞏᏕᎱ	Appearance
ᏕᎱᏕᎱ	various appearances
ᏕᎱᎱ	to look
ᏕᎱᎱᏕᎱ	is looking
ᏕᏒᎱᏙᏕ	Happiness
ᏕᎱᏒᏙᏕᏒᏙᏕ	is skipping for joy
ᏕᏕᏒ	Skeleton
ᏕᏕᏕᏒ	various skeletons
ᏕᎱᏕᏕᏕᏒ	is becoming a skeleton
ᏒᎱᎱᎱ	to buy
ᏙᏒᏔᎱ	Summit
ᏙᏒᎱᏔᎱ	to reach the top

11.2.

ᏕᎱᏕᏒ	to become a skeleton
ᏙᏒᏔᏙᏒᏔᎱ	various summits
ᏙᏒᎱᏔᏙᏒᏔᎱ	is reaching the top
ᏒᎱᎱᎱ	(the/a) purchase
ᏒᎱᎱᎱᏒᎱᎱᎱ	is buying

11.3. The first step is to divide the English items into semantically similar groups, and the Baybayin items into groups based on shared symbols. We then deduce that the group including ᏕᎱ must correspond to the "look/appearances" group (four members each), ᏕᏕᏒ must correspont to the "skeleton" group (three members each), and ᏒᎱᎱᎱ must be "to buy." We also need to figure out the nature of the Baybayin alternations, which include two basic processes:

- From the basic form, copy the initial two symbols and add them to the beginning. The first symbol retains its diacritic, whereas the diacritic of the second symbol is replaced by a cross below.

- Insert Ꮁ as the second symbol, move the diacritic of the initial symbol to Ꮁ, and add an underdot to the first symbol.

(12) Spare the Rod (1/3)

12.1. X1. Little Red Riding Hood: Grandmother, why do you have such big eyes? (Or, "Grandmother, why are your eyes so big?")
X2. "Grandmother": To be able to see you better, my child.

The only reasonable way to solve part 1 completely was to see similarities to the story of the Little Red Riding Hood. We can detect these similarities based on the repetitive structure, impersonation suggested by the quotes around "mormor," and similarity of the word "Rødhette" to "Red Hood."

12.2.

X3 – Y1	unaligned – Y5
X4 – Y2	unaligned – Y6
X1 – Y3	X5 – Y7
X2 – Y4	X6 – Y8

Easy observations
- The text is a dialogue, and each even-numbered sentence answers the preceding odd-numbered sentence in text X. Thus, each even-numbered sentence in text Y should match the preceding odd-numbered sentence.
- Sentence pairs Y1–Y2, Y3–Y4, Y5–Y6, and Y7–Y8 differ only in two words each: ører/høre, øyne/se, hender/klemme, and munn/ete. Similarly, pairs X1–X2, X3–X4, and X5–X6 differ only in ögon/se, öron/höra, and tänder/kunna äta upp dig.
- Since ører matches öron by regular sound changes, høre matches höra, se matches se, and kunna äta matches kunna ete, the matching sentences are X4–Y2, X1–Y3, X2–Y4, and X6–Y8.
- Since each even-numbered sentence answers the preceding odd-numbered sentence, X3 must match Y1, and X5 must match Y7, leaving Y5 and Y6 unaligned. A common mistake is to assume that tänder matches hender, but it is a less plausible sound change, and it does not fit the structure of the story.

12.3. Most pairs of words are related by a small number of regular sound changes, such as a/e in kunna/kunne, and ö/ø and a/e in höra/høre, so we can match them as follows:

så–så	har–har	skall–skal	bättre–bedre
stora–store	det–det	kunna–kunne	se–se
öron–ører	är– er	höra–høre	äte–ete
du–du	jag–jeg	dig–deg	

This initial matching does not include the words bestemor, Rødhette, fordi, svarte, ulven, øyne, hender, klemme, stor, and munn.

- Rødhette and Rödluvan are the only proper nouns, so we can match them.

(12) Spare the Rod (2/3)

- Part 2 shows that *øyne* matches *ögon*, and that *hender* and *klemme* are unmatched; the scoring did not account for the matching of *munn* (mouth) and *tänder* (teeth).
- *stor* is the singular form of *store*, but the scoring did not account for it.
- "*så Rødhette*" indicates *Rødhette*'s speech in text Y, which serves the same function as "*Rödluvan:*" in text X. Therefore, "*svarte ulven*" in text Y indicates speech, just as "*Mormor:*" in text X; note that "*svarte ulven*" does not match "*mitt barn.*"
- The commas indicate that *Rödluvan* addresses "*men mormor,*" whereas *Rødhette* addresses "*bestemor,*" which implies that *bestemor* matches *mormor*.
- Finally, *fordi* matches *för att*.

12.4. The problem scoring accounted only for *har, sa, det, er, jeg*, and *kunne*. We can guess their meaning based on the sound similarity, since the respective English words are related to languages X and Y by regular sound changes, or based on the knowledge of the story, or based on cognates in other Germanic languages. Also, it is possible to match some of these words based on more distantly related Indo-European languages, such as French. Note that, although the knowledge of the story about the Little Red Riding Hood may help solving this problem, it is essential only for solving part 1. Everything else in this problem can be solved through logical deduction.

Language X	Language Y	English
så	så	such
stora	store	large (plural)
öron	ører	ears
du	du	you (subject)
har	har	**have**
mormor	bestemor	grandmother
—	sa	**said**
Rödluvan	Rødhette	(Little) Red (Riding) Hood
det	det	**they**
är	er	**are**
för att	fordi	for
jag	jeg	**I**
skall	skal	shall
kunna	kunne	**can**
höra	høre	hear
dig	deg	you (object)

(12) Spare the Rod (3/3)

bättre	bedre	better
—-	svarte	answered
—-	ulven	the wolf
ögon	øyne	eyes
se	se	see
—-	hender	hands
—-	klemme	hug
—-	stor	large (singular)
—-	munn	mouth
äta	ete	eat

12.5. Explanations for parts 1-4 have been given above.

12.6. The overlap between the vocabularies of X and Y is much larger than the overlap between them and English. Also, the sound changes between X and Y are smaller than between them and English. Thus, they are more closely related to each other than to English. They are both Germanic languages; specifically, X is Swedish, and Y is Norwegian.

(13) A Fish Story (1/1)

13.1. Here are the correct matches:

g 1. *"Mä hach'a challwawa challwataxa."*
b 2. *"Kimsa hach'a challwawa challwataxa."* **(lie)**
a 3. *"Mä challwa mä hach'a challwampiwa challwataxa."*
c 4. *"Mä hach'a challwa kimsa challwallampiwa challwataxa."*
d 5. *"Paya challwallawa challwataxa."*
f 6. *"Mä challwalla paya challwampiwa challwataxa."*
e 7. *"Kimsa challwa paya challwallampiwa challwataxa."*

13.2. There are two possible correct answers:

Kimsa challwalla paya hach'a challwampiwa challwataxa.
Paya hach'a challwa kimsa challwallampiwa challwataxa.

13.3. We need to notice the following patterns in order to solve this problem:

- *challwataxa* is the last word of each sentence, which may mean "caught" or "fished."
- *mä, paya,* and *kimsa* are the numbers.
- *challwa* is the root "fish."
- *–lla* indicates the little fish, whereas *hach'a* indicates the big fish.
- *–mpi* occurs whenever there are two kinds of fish.
- *–wa* occurs at the very end, but before *challwataxa.*

(14) Fakepapershelfmaker (1/2)

14.1. (a) *nisetanukijiru*   fake soup made out of raccoons
       (b) *nisedanukijiru*   soup made out of fake raccoons
       (c) *irogamibako*   box for colored paper
       (d) *irokamibako*   colored box for paper
       (e) *nisezakuradana*   shelf for fake cherry blossoms
       (f) *nisesakuradana*   fake shelf for cherry blossoms

14.2. (1) a fake shelf-maker made of paper   B: *nisekamitanadzukuri*
       (2) a maker of fake shelves for paper   D: *nisekamidanadzukuri*
       (3) a fake maker of shelves for paper   D: *nisekamidanadzukuri*
       (4) a shelf-maker made of fake paper   C: *nisegamitanadzukuri*
       (5) a maker of shelves for fake paper   A: *nisegamidanadzukuri*

14.3. When we compound two Japanese words, the first word modifies/describes the second. For example, adding *hashi* before *hako* makes a word meaning a box (*hako*) for chopsticks (*hashi*). As another example, adding *nuri* before *hashi* makes a word meaning chopsticks (*hashi*) that are lacquered (*nuri*).

Every simple (non-compound) word has two forms: the basic form, used when it occurs alone, and the variant form, sometimes used in compound words.

Basic	Variant	Basic	Variant
hako	<u>b</u>ako	shiru	<u>j</u>iru
hana	<u>b</u>ana	Sora	<u>z</u>ora
hashi	<u>B</u>ashi	tana	<u>d</u>ana
kami	<u>g</u>ami	tanuki	<u>d</u>anuki
kiri	<u>g</u>iri	tsukuri	<u>dz</u>ukuri
sakura	<u>z</u>akura		

The variant form has a different first letter, which depends on the first letter in the basic form. Specifically, we replace the initial *h* with *b*, initial *k* with *g*, initial *s* with *z*, initial *sh* with *j*, initial *t* with *d*, and initial *ts* with *dz*. As a side note, some letters do not require replacement, but they do not occur in the problem.

We next deduce rules for compounding simple words; we denote basic forms by *a, b, c,* and *d*, and respective variants by <u>*a*</u>, <u>*b*</u>, <u>*c*</u>, and <u>*d*</u>. We first notice that two-member compounds have the following structure:

$$a + b \rightarrow a\underline{b}$$

Three-member compounds have two different structures, which depend on their meaning. If we first form a

(14) Fakepapershelfmaker (2/2)

word containing *a* and *b*, and then compound it with *c*, we use the following structure:

$$(a + b) + c \rightarrow a\underline{b} + c \rightarrow ab\underline{c}$$

If we first compound *b* and *c*, and then add *c*, we use a different structure:

$$a + (b + c) \rightarrow a + b\underline{c} \rightarrow ab\underline{c}$$

Thus, when we combine two (simple or compound) words into a larger compound word, we use the following rules:

- We use the original form of the first word.
- If the second word is simple (noncompound), we use its variant form.
- If the second word is compound, we do not change it.

When compounding four simple words, we can get five different internal structures; two of them give the same result, which is why the four compounds in part 2 correspond to five possible meanings.

We can now determine which English version corresponds to what structure.

(1) **a fake shelf-maker made of paper**
→ fake + (paper + (shelf + maker))
→ a + (b + (c + d))
→ a + (b + c<u>d</u>)
→ a + bc<u>d</u>
→ abc<u>d</u>
→ ***nise-kami-tana-dzukiri*** (B)

(2) **a maker of fake shelves for paper**
→ (fake + (paper + shelf)) + maker
→ (a + (b + <u>c</u>)) + d
→ (a + b<u>c</u>) + d
→ ab<u>c</u> + d
→ ab<u>cd</u>
→ ***nise-kami-dana-dzukuri*** (D)

(3) **a fake maker of shelves for paper**
→ fake + ((paper + shelf) + maker)
→ a + ((b + c) + d)
→ a + (bc + d)
→ a + b<u>cd</u>
→ ab<u>cd</u>
→ **nise-kami-dana-dzukuri** (D)

(4) **a shelf-maker made of fake paper**
→ (a + b) + (c + d)
→ a<u>b</u> + c<u>d</u>
→ ab<u>cd</u>
→ ***nise-gami-tana-dzukuri*** (C)

(5) **a maker of shelves for fake paper**
→ ((a + b) + c) + d
→ (a<u>b</u> + c) + d
→ (ab<u>c</u>) + d
→ ab<u>cd</u>
→ ***nise-gami-dana-dzukuri*** (A)

(15) Manam, I'm Anam (1/2)

15.1. A: *Pita*   B: *Butokang*   C: *Sulung*   D: *Tola*   E: *Sala*

15.2. 1. *Arongo pera kana ilau ieno, Butokang pera kana auta ieno.*
           2. *Arongo pera kana awa ieno, Pita pera kana ata ieno.*
           3. *Arongo pera kana awa ilau ieno, Sulung pera kana ata auta ieno.*

15.3.   The analysis of the given examples suggests that *auta, ilau, ata,* and *awa* are the significant words, which probably represent directions. For reference, "X *pera kana*" means "X's house", and *ieno* means "is located." We can see that *auta* and *ilau* appear to be opposed, and that *ata* and *awa* are also opposed. We thus hypothesize that they represent two axes of dimensions, and we support this hypothesis by observing that their compounds are intermediate directions, such as *awa ilau* vs. *ata auta*, and *awa auta* vs. *ata ilau*. In fact, these compounds may occur in either order; for example, *ilau awa* and *auta ata* are also directions. *Ilau awa* is similar but not identical to *awa ilau*, in the same way as "north-north-west" is similar but not identical to "west-north-west."

When we analyze the relative locations of the houses of Onkau, Kulu, and Mombwa, we may be tempted to assume that *auta* is North, *ilau* is South, *awa* is East, and *ata* is West. This assumption works until about half-way through the problem, but then we should notice contradictions: either these directions are very imprecise or some houses are in the sea. When we reach a contradiction, we should try discarding some of the underlying assumptions; in this case, we discard the assumption that the islanders reckon the traditional directions, that is, North, South, East, and West. Instead, we should consider other directional possibilities that may occur to the islanders.

In fact, *auta* means "inland" or "upland," which is the same thing on a cone-shaped volcanic island, and *ilau* means "seaward." Furthermore, *Ata* means "clockwise around the island," and *awa* means "counterclockwise". The compound direction *awa auta* thus means "inland in a counterclockwise direction".

An alternative approach to solving this problem is as follows. We may be fairly certain that the directions form two axes, *auta/ilau* and *ata/awa*. Instead of placing islanders on the given map, as soon as we have a hunch where they live, we can work out an abstract two-dimensional map indicating the relative locations of the houses. Then, by comparing it to the given map, we can see that the only way to reconcile the two maps is to "wrap" the abstract map around the island, that is, to curve the Cartesian grid of houses into a polar grid centered on the volcano.

(15) Manam, I'm Anam (2/2)

The full Manam compass rose is as follows:

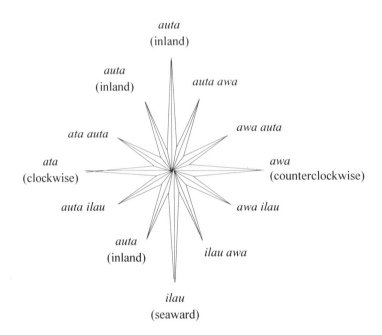

Note that some of the directions are irrelevant to the problem, and we have included them only for completeness. Also note that the angle between *auta* and North depends on a specific location, which means that this compass would rotate with respect to the traditional North/South compass as we walk around the island. If you have solved this difficult problem, you are probably able to examine and revise your initial assumptions, which is an essential research skill.

(16) Thorny Stems (1/1)

1. If a word ends in *ies*, then replace *ies* with **y**. Exception: **series**
2. If a word ends in *ss*, then replace *ss* with **ss**. No exceptions
3. If a word ends in *ives*, then replace *ves* with **fe**. Exception: **hives**
4. If a word ends in *ves*, then replace *ves* with **f**. Exception: **caves**
5. If a word ends in *oes*, then replace *oes* with **o**. Exception: **floes**
6. If a word ends in *s*, then replace *s* with ___. Exception: **guesses**
7. If a word ends in *ing*, then replace *ing* with ___. Exception: **closing**
8. If a word ends in *ied*, then replace *ied* with **y**. Exception: **lied**
9. If a word ends in *ed*, then replace *ed* with ___. Exception: **posed**
10. Otherwise the word is its own stem. Exception: **formulae**

We may find multiple exceptions to most rules; some examples are as follows:
- Rule 5: toes
- Rule 6: bus
- Rule 7: ring
- Rule 9: bed

The order of rules is somewhat flexible, and the only requirements are as follows:
- Rules 1–5 are before Rule 6.
- Rule 3 is before Rule 4.
- Rule 8 is before Rule 9.

Notes and common mistakes

- The word "wives" has a unique pattern, which requires its own rule (Rule 3).
- We need Rule 2 so that Rule 6 does not remove *s* from words like "moss."
- A common mistake is to list more specific cases after more general cases, such as Rule 8 after Rule 9. Since we use the first matching rule, this ordering leads to ignoring the appropriate specific rule.
- An additional rule for the words ending in **es** is not required in the given rule set, since these words match either Rules 3–5 or Rule 6.
- A word is an exception only if the entire rule set gives a wrong result for this word. For example, "knives" is not an exception to Rule 4, because it matches Rule 3, which is before Rule 4.
- The problem statement does not allow the use of wildcards or other complex specifications; for example, we cannot collapse Rules 1 and 8 to a single *ie** rule, and we also cannot define a single rule for the words ending in **<consonant>ves**.

(17) aw-TOM-uh-tuh (1/1)

17.1.   Possible: *iu, oire, urioo, raorao, uaia*
Impossible: *idau, uente, voav, oratreopaveiepa*

17.2.

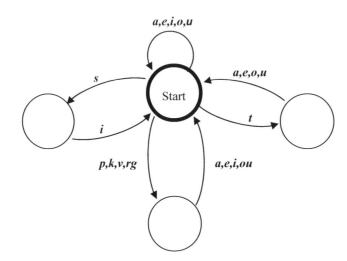

17.3.   The letters *t* and *s* have restrictions on their use before vowels, which makes them different from the other consonants. We can use *s* only before *i*; for example, "sisigarue" is a valid word, whereas "uasau" is invalid. Furthermore, we cannot use *t* before *i*, which means that we can use it only before *a*, *e*, *o*, and *u*; for example, "kotoe" is a valid word, whereas "tiravau" is invalid. This observation implies a special relationship between *t* and *s*; in fact, it suggests that these two sounds are the same on an abstract level, although their pronunciation and spelling depends on the following vowel.

(18) The Curragh of Kildare (1/3)

18.1.

	English	Irish	Translation
20	Mullaghbane	*An Mullach Bán*	*The White Summit*
21	Killananny	*Cill an Eanaigh/Coill an Eanaigh*	Church of the Fen/ Wood of the Fen
22	Knocknakillardy	*Cnoc na Cille Airde/ Cnoc na Coille Airde*	*Hill of the High Church/ Hill of the High Wood*
23	Gortnabinna	*Gort na Binne*	*Field of the Peak*
24	Clashgortmore	*Clais an Ghoirt Mhóir*	*Pit of the Big Field*
25	Killbeg	*An Chill Bheag/An Choill Bheag*	*The Small Church/The Small Wood*
26	Blackcastle	*An Caisleán Dubh*	Black castle

18.2. A number of observations can be made.

Orthographic correspondences: The English names are phonetic imitations of the Irish names. The letter correspondences (Irish/English) include *c/k*, *ch/gh*, and *aigh/y*, but many Irish letters do not have English equivalents; for example, there is no distinction between *cill* and *coill*.

Irish place names: The names fit the following pattern, where brackets represent optional parts; note that adjectives come after the respective nouns:

[An] <noun-1> [<adjective-1>] [an/na <noun-2> [<adjective-2>]]

If a name includes a second noun, it is in the "of" form, which is analogous to the "<noun>'s" form in English, such as "John's." If it includes an adjective after the "of" noun, this adjective is also in the "of" form. Furthermore, an article before the "of" noun is sometimes *na*, rather than *an*. We can identify the related patterns by comparing the two forms.

Nouns:

Base Form	"Of" Form	Translation
gort	an ghoirt	field
an currach	an churraigh	marsh
an pháirc/páirc	na páirce	park
cill	na cille	church
an choill	na coille	wood
an bun/ bun	?	base
an bhinn	?	peak
baile	?	town

(18) The Curragh of Kildare (2/3)

Base Form	"Of" Form	Translation
cluain	?	meadow
gleann	?	valley
eanach	?	fen
an dún	?	ford
talamh	?	land
an mhainistir	?	abbey
an chlais	?	pit
?	na muice	pig
?	an mhullaigh	summit
?	an uain	lamb
?	an chairn	mound
?	an chaisleáin	castle
?	an chnoic	hill

We notice two classes of nouns.

Class A: The nouns whose last vowel is *i*.
- Insert –h– in the base form when preceded by the article.
- Add –e in the end to construct the "of" form.
- Use the article *na* in the "of" form.

Class B: The nouns whose last vowel is not *i*.
- No changes in the base form.
- Add –i– before the last consonant cluster to construct the "of" form.
- Use the article *an* and insert –h– after the first consonant in the "of" form.

(18) The Curragh of Kildare (3/3)

Adjectives: The behavior of an adjective depends on the class of the related noun.

Base form		"Of" form		Translation
Class A	Class B	Class A	Class B	
	dhubh		duibhe	black
	bhán	bháin		white
ard				high
	íseal			low
mór	mhór			big
beag				small

An adjective after a Class A noun behaves like a Class A noun with an article. Similarly, an adjective after a Class B noun behaves like a Class B noun with an article.

English place names: The Irish words always have the same English correspondence, regardless of their grammatical form, with the exception of the –ach/–aigh words; for example, bán, bháin, bhán, and báine all correspond to –bane in an English name.

(19) Tzolk'in (1/2)

19.1. a. 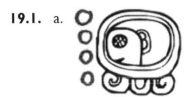 b.

19.2. c. — August 23
d. — September 19

19.3. Every 260 days.

19.4. We first observe that each day name includes two glyphs, which repeat in cycles of different length. In particular, the right-hand side glyphs, which look like little pictures, repeat every twenty days. For example, the 🜨 glyph reappears three times: August 18, September 7, and September 27; as a side note, it means "Venus". Thus, the picture glyphs should repeat either every 20 days, or in some shorter cycle that is a divisor of 20; however, if we consider all smaller divisors of 20, we find out that they cause "collisions" between glyphs, which means that the length of the cycle is exactly 20. As another side note, there is no way to identify the beginning of this cycle, and Mayans do not have a general consensus about its "start" day.

On the other hand, the glyphs on the left appear to cycle every 13 days:

We find three missing glyphs in parts 2 and 3, and we can use the observed pattern to put them in their proper places. We can also deduce the positions of days in parts 2c and 3d, which increases the certainty of placing the dot-and-bar glyphs.

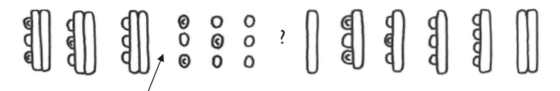

We can determine the "start" for this sequence by observing the pattern of these glyphs; specifically, the arrow above shows the discontinuity in the pattern, which is likely to be the start of the cycle, thus leading to the following order:

(19) Tzolk'in (2/2)

We next observe that (1) the third glyph consists of three empty circles, and (2) the eighth glyph has three circles, the ninth has four circles, and the tenth has an extra bar instead of the circles. In fact, these symbols are numbers, and we can deduce their representation; specifically, a number is a sum of its elements, where an empty circle is 1 and a bar is 5. We can thus deduce that the fourth glyph consists of four empty circles:

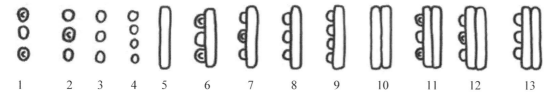

We can now determine most day names.

In particular, September 28 (part 1a) is as shown on the left, since it is immediately after a "3" day, and it is 40 days after August 19, which should have the same picture glyph.

The only places for glyphs in parts 2c and 2d are on August 23 and September 19, which gives the positions of 19 out of the 20 picture glyphs, and leaves only one missing picture glyph.

The day in part 1b falls on one of the missing-glyph days. We next note that the missing picture glyph appear in part 3, and thus it should be as shown on the left.

In conclusion, we observe that the lengths of the two cycles, 20 and 13, are relatively prime, which means that the length of the combined cycle is 20 x 13 = 260 days, and thus the Tzolk'in year is 260 days long. Note that it serves only as the ritual calendar, and not as the agricultural calendar.

(20) The Whole Spectrum (1/2)

20.1. 13: Lease   14: Ash   15: Sheep   16: Louse

20.2.

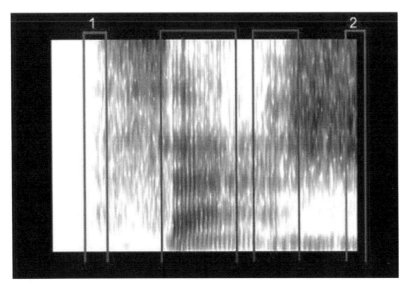

Each left endpoint is correct if it is inside box 1, and each right endpoint is correct if it is inside box 2. Ideally, there should be significant overlap between the intervals affected by /s/ and /a/.

20.3.

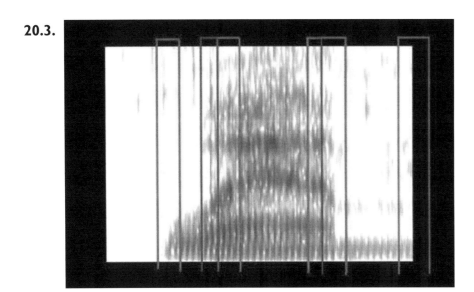

As above. The intervals for /l/ and /a/ must overlap or be adjacent, and the intervals for /a/ and /m/ must overlap, since the /m/ nasalizes the end of the preceding /a/.

(20) The Whole Spectrum (2/2)

20.4. When the same basic sound, which is called *phoneme*, occurs in multiple words, it has similar effects. In particular, *s* and *sh* have distinctive appearances, and the vowels have distinctive sets of bars, which are called *formants*. These formants are effected by adjacent consonants in most cases (in fact, some consonants, called *stop consonants* (e.g., *p* and *k*) can be distinguished only this way, hence the seeming lack of a /p/ after "sheep"), which suffices to identify the first three spectrograms. Note that the apparent shifting of the formants in the first one does not indicate a diphthong, but is simply a glide from /i/ to /j/. Also, the difference between /i/ (lease) and /ai/ (lice) is only an initial /a/, so the similarity between the end of, say, "ice" or "mice" and spectrogram 13 is not relevant. The vowel in the last one is not one shown in the previous spectrograms: just as /ai/ (as in "mice" or "shine") shifts from /a/ to /i/, the vowel in the last spectrogram shifts from /a/ to /u/. The English vowel with this property is /au/, so the last spectrogram is of "*louse*."

20.5. Vowels clearly affect particularly long intervals, as do the sibilants *s* and *sh*, which can be said both continuously and loudly. Nasals after vowels also affect long intervals, because they nasalize the preceding vowels. Transitions between sounds are not instantaneous, since the mouth changes smoothly from one position to another, so "intervals" have at least some level of imprecision.

For most sounds in this problem, transitions were fairly abrupt, but others, e.g., final stops (initial stops are visible by their aspiration, an initial region of high amplitude) are detectable mostly by their effects on adjacent vowels, although they seem to have no intervals to themselves. With this observation in mind, it is possible to postulate another stop consonant at the start of vowel-initial words, and careful pronunciation of them does indeed reveal an unwritten glottal stop.

In the given spectrograms, a glottal stop is present in every vowel-initial word except *e* (the beginning of *e* in the given spectrograms is simply a matter of amplitude). Also, some diphthongs are arguably not indicated, and the glides that come after English long vowels, such that /j/ after /i/ and /w/ after /u/, are not indicated, but clearly visible at the end of, say, "knee." Conversely, certain letters of English orthography are not pronounced at all, such as final silent *e*, the initial *k* in "knee," the final *b* in "lamb," the doubled letters in words like "coo," and other vowel combinations. Most of these were pronounced at one point in the history of English, but as pronunciations changed, the orthography did not follow it.

(21) Tenji Karaoke (1/2)

The first step to solving this problem is to notice that there are 4 different characters in the tenji for **karaoke**, each corresponding to a syllable in the word (ka-ra-o-ke). Thus, the easiest way to go about starting the problem is to look for words that have the same syllables in them as the word **karaoke**. From the "ka" in karaoke, one can deduce that letter C is **katana**, because it begins with the same syllable as karaoke.

karaoke

c.

Using this same method, we can deduce that b. is **sake**, because the last syllable matches the last syllable of **karaoke**. Because we know **katana**, we can figure out that f. is **atari**, because the second syllable is the same.

Now there are no more syllables in common with each other. However, it is noticeable that many of the words in this data set have the letter "k" in them (We are including k- syllables that we have not solved yet to better illustrate the example. It is possible to do this with the three we already know).

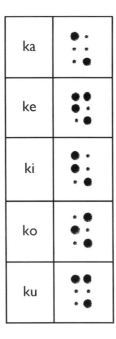

(21) Tenji Karaoke (2/2)

When looking at this data set, the thing all of these syllables have in common is their bottom two dots and the left dot on the second row. We can infer from this that the characters are bisected diagonally between consonants and vowels. Take a look at all of the syllables without consonants:

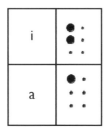

Knowing this, it is very easy now to go through and solve the rest of the words comparing the syllables to those you already know.

21.1. **a.** haiku   **b.** sake
         c. katana   **d.** kimono
         e. koi   **f.** atari

To do Part 2, you go backwards: you recognize **ka** from **karaoke**, then you figure out the rest of the word by looking at the two parts of each syllable and comparing them to those in the words you've already figured out.

21.2. **a.** karate   **b.** anime

To do Part 3, you write the symbols using the same method, being careful to notice that **samurai** has four syllables and the last syllable is simply "i".

21.3. **a.**

           b.

(22) Nok-nok! (1/1)

The spelling tutor computes the EDIT DISTANCE between the given word spelling and the correct spelling. We use the standard definition of operations required for converting one of the two given strings into the other, where each operation is one of the following three:

- Removal of a letter.
- Insertion of a letter (anywhere in the string).
- Replacement of a letter with (any other) letter.

The spelling tutor converts the edit distance into a comment using the following scheme:

Distance	Comment
0	no comment; correct
1	almost right
2	quite close
3	a bit confusing
4	very confusing

The examples given in the problem do NOT show comments for the edit distance of 5 or more, because Christopher Robin never makes so many mistakes, not even in long and delicate words.

The edit distances and related comments for the given misspellings of "typo" are as follows:

Misspelled Text	Distance	Comment
oooo	3	a bit confusing
opyt	4	very confusing
pyto	2	quite close
typ	1	almost right
typa	1	almost right
typotypo	4	very confusing

(23) Letters for Cuzco (1/2)

23.1. [q] and [χ] never occur in the same position:

- [q] is *always* before a vowel,
- [χ] is *never* before a vowel; it only appears before other consonants and at the end of the word.

(Another way of saying this is "[q] always occurs at the beginning of syllables, and [χ] only occurs at the end of syllables".)

If we represent these by the same letter—for example, <q>— we'll always know whether it's meant to be pronounced [q] or [χ] based on whether or not it's followed by a vowel.

23.2. If [a] and [i] were represented by the same letter, then [qasa] ("frost") and [qasi] ("free") would be written identically, and a reader wouldn't be able to determine from the written form which word was meant.

This is also true for [karu] ("far") and [kiru] ("teeth").

This violates a rule of orthography design—that given a written word, there should be no question of how to pronounce it.

23.3. Like in part 2, if [a] and [e] were represented by the same letter, then [saqey] ("to abandon") and [seqay] ("to climb") would be written identically, and a reader would be unable to distinguish them. This again violates our second rule of orthography design.

23.4. First, we can establish which vowels *can't* be represented by a single letter. Above, we proved that [a] and [i] can't be combined, nor can [a] and [e].

- The pair [kisa] ("nettle") and [kisu] ("cheese") shows that [a] and [u] can't be combined; so does the pair [kanka] ("roasted") and [kunka] ("neck").
- The pair [qasa] ("frost") and [qosa] ("husband") shows that [a] and [o] can't be combined.
- The pair [kisa] ("nettle") and [kusa] ("great") shows that [i] and [u] can't be combined.

Having ruled these out, our only option is to somehow combine [e] and [o] with [i] and [u]. Meanwhile, we can notice that [e] and [o] *only* occur in a specific environment (next to a [q]/[χ]), whereas [i] and [u] *never* occur in this environment. This will allow us to combine [e] with either [i] or [u], and [o] with either [i] or [u], while still allowing the reader to predict how the letter should be pronounced. Given what we know so far, there are two possibilities of how to do this:

(23) Letters for Cuzco (2/2)

- <u>Possibility 1:</u> Represent [i] and [e] as a single letter, which is pronounced [e] when it's next to [q/χ] and [i] otherwise, and then represent [u] and [o] as a single letter, which is pronounced [o] when it's next to [q]/[χ] and [u] otherwise.

- <u>Possibility 2:</u> Represent [u] and [e] as a single letter, which is pronounced [e] when it's next to [q]/[χ] and [u] otherwise, and then represent [i] and [o] as a single letter, which is pronounced [o] when it's next to [q]/[χ] and [i] otherwise.

Both of these solutions work, but there's a pattern in the words given that makes Possibility 1 a more compelling choice:

qelqaχ	writer	**qatoχ**	merchant	**sipeχ**	murderer
qelqay	to write	**qatuy**	to barter	**sipiy**	to kill

In each of these, the word ending in [y] is the action, whereas the word ending in [χ] is a person who does that action. When we replace a [y] with an [χ] in [qelqa-], nothing happens to the preceding vowel, but for the other words, there's a vowel change.

That [u] "changes" to [o] when an [χ] is introduced, and that [i] "changes" to [e] when an [χ] is introduced, is good reason to believe that [u] should match with [o], and [i] with [e]. Possibility 1 lets us represent this pattern very easily: if [u]/[o] and [i]/[e] are each represented with one letter, the only thing that changes is the [χ] and [y], making the pattern for "barter" and "kill" the same as that for "write".

If you've come to the same answer, then congratulations! You've just worked out the modern Cuzco Quechua orthography using only 33 words and your wits. For reference, current practice uses:

- <q> to represent [q] before a vowel and [χ] elsewhere.
- <i> to represent [e] when next to <q>, and [i] elsewhere.
- <u> to represent [o] when next to <q>, and [u] elsewhere

(24) You will be laughing (1/1)

The Guaraní verb consists of:

1. prefix **n(d)(a)-**, if negation exists;
2. person and number of the subject: **a-** 'I', **o-** 'he', **ja-** 'we', **pe-** 'you (pl.)';
3. root;
4. **-(r)i**, if negation exists;
5. ending **-ma** for past tense or **-ta** for future tense.

where:

- the negative prefix should start with **n** (rather than **nd**) in case the root of the verb contains any nasal sound (nasal sounds include **m**, **n**);
- the vowel **a** is dropped from the negative prefix in case the personal prefix starts with a vowel;
- if a future tense is to be negated, the suffix is **-mo'ãi,** rather than *-(r)i-ta*; the negative suffix is **-ri** after the vowel **I**; **-i** otherwise.

24.1.   (a) I was eating.
        (b) He will be waking up.
        (c) I will not be taking.
        (d) You are not crying
        (e) I wasn't catching.

24.2.   (f) ne-pe-mbokapu-i
        (g) ndo-purahei-ri
        (h) ja-karu-ta
        (i) nda-purahei-mo'ãi

(25) Summer Eyes (1/1)

An extractive summarizer scores each sentence according to a set of criteria. Then it picks the top 3 sentences from each story based on the sum of its scores on the different criteria.

The first criterion is *primacy*. The first sentence gets 3 points, the second 2, and the third 1, to account for the likely increased importance of the initial sentences. Then multiples of .1 are added, starting with .0, for the last sentence, to break the other criteria's ties in favor of earlier sentences.
The second criterion is *recency*. The last sentence gets 3 points, the second to last, 2, and the antepenultimate, 1, to account for the fact that they're likely "summary-ish" themselves.
The third criterion counts *named entities* in the sentence, since they're likely to describe the most important actors.
The fourth criterion counts *words from the title* that appear in the sentence (after reducing each word to a stem; e.g., struck = strike). These sentences are likely to pertain most immediately to the topic of the story.
The fifth criterion counts *named entities introduced for the first time* in this sentence. The first mention of a named entity is probably important for understanding its role.
The sixth criterion counts *past-tense verbs*. Current information is probably more important, and past-tense verbs are slightly less likely to give new information.

25.1.

Story 1, sentence 2, criterion 3 - change to 1
Story 1, sentence 2, criterion 5 - change to 1
Story 1, sentence 2, total - change to 2.3

Story 1, sentence 5, criterion 3 - change to 0
Story 1, sentence 5, total - change to 3.0

Story 2, sentence 1, criterion 1 - change to 3.9
Story 2, sentence 1, total - change to 8.9

Story 2, sentence 2, criterion 1 - change to 2.8
Story 2, sentence 2, total - change to 4.8

Story 2, sentence 3, criterion 1 - change to 0.6 (similarly change the next 6 numbers down from this one to be 0.1 less than before)
Story 2, sentence 2, total - change to 2.6 (this affects the totals for the next 6 sentences)

Story 2, sentence 5, criterion 5 - change to 2
Story 2, sentence 5, total - change to 4.4

Story 2, sentence 8, criterion 5 - change to 1
Story 2, sentence 8, total - change to 4.1

25.2. 1.7 0 2 3 2 -4 4.7

(26) Help my camera! (1/1)

26.1. Ex1: *it*   Ex2: *him*   Ex3: *them*

26.2 The computer interprets pronouns as referring to the last noun phrase in the previous sentence.

26.3. There are many possible answers. Some examples are:

- Interpret pronouns as referring to the previous sentence's first noun.

- Interpret pronouns as referring to a noun in the previous sentence with the same number/gender properties.

- Interpret pronouns as referring to the previous sentence's subject.

- Check for sentences of parallel syntactic structure first, and refer to a noun (phrase) in the same place if there is one.

(27) Sk8 Parsr (1/3)

27.1. ↓←↑△→↓◎▣↓←↑△→↓◎↑↑

27.2. ▣⊗▣↓▣⊗↑▣↓▣⊗▣↓▣⊗↑↑

If the right side of the input matches…		*Replace it with…*
a.	← ↑ △	⟹ **Backside-180**
b.	→ ↓ ◎	⟹ **Frontside-180**
c.	▣ ⊗	⟹ **Ollie**
d.	⊗ ▣	⟹ **Nollie**
e.	**Nollie ▣ Ollie**	⟹ **Woolie**
f.	↓ ↓	⟹ **Crouch**
g.	**Backside-180 Frontside-180**	⟹ **Backside-360**
h.	**Crouch Backside-360**	⟹ **360-Kickflip**
i.	↓ a ↑	⟹ **Inverted-a**
j.	a ▣ a	⟹ **Double-a**
k.	**Double-a ▣ a**	⟹ **Triple-a**
l.	**Double-a ▣ Double-a**	⟹ **Quadruple-a**
m.	a ▣ **Inverted-a**	⟹ **Atomic-a**

132

27.4. Consider the sequence of button presses that would make up a Quadruple-Ollie (or Quadruple-anything).

⊙⊗⊙⊙⊗⊙⊙⊗⊙⊙⊗

Considering each button in turn, the parser first turns the first two symbols into an Ollie, then that and the subsequent Ollie into a Double-Ollie:

1. ⊙
2. ⊙ ⊗
3. Ollie
4. Ollie ⊙
5. Ollie ⊙ ⊙
6. Ollie ⊙ ⊙ ⊗
7. Ollie ⊙ Ollie
8. Double-Ollie

When the parser comes across the next Ollie, it then combines it with the previous Double-Ollie to make a Triple-Ollie:

9. Double-Ollie ⊙
10. Double-Ollie ⊙ ⊙
11. Double-Ollie ⊙ ⊙ ⊗
12. Double-Ollie ⊙ Ollie
13. Triple-Ollie

However, there's no way to turn a Triple-Ollie into a Quadruple-Ollie. You can never get a sequence that runs Double-Ollie ⊙ Double-Ollie, because the first half of the second Double-Ollie would have already combined with the previous symbols to create a Triple-Ollie. This sequence of buttons can only produce Triple-Ollie ⊙:

14. Triple-Ollie ⊙
15. Triple-Ollie ⊙ ⊙
16. Triple-Ollie ⊙ ⊙ ⊗
17. Triple-Ollie ⊙ Ollie

In order to make a Quadruple-Ollie possible, then, we should rewrite the Quadruple-**a** rule so that:

Triple-**a** ⊙ **a** → Quadruple-**a**

(27) Sk8 Parsr (3/3)

27.5. There are a large (in fact, infinite) number of possible combos that the parser can never actually parse, due to the fact that it recognizes some sub-sequence of the combo as a different combo and reduces it, rendering that sub-sequence unusable by the original rule.

For example, you can never perform a Double-Nollie (or any further iteration of Nollies), because the parser recognizes a spurious Ollie inside of it:

⊗▣▣⊗▢ → Nollie Ollie ▢

Likewise, *any* Inverted-Inverted-a, as well as anything built on it (like an Atomic-Inverted-a), will fail, because the parser always recognizes two consecutive ↓'s as a Crouch:

↓↓ a ↑↑ → crouch a ↑↑

The same goes for any sort of Inversion of a Crouch or any move beginning in a Crouch, such as the Inverted-360-Kickflip. The first ↓, which should be part of the Inversion part, is instead reduced along with the first ↓ of the Crouch to make a spurious Crouch, and the leftovers are interpreted incorrectly as an Inverted-Backside-360:

↓↓↓←↑△→↓◎↑ → crouch ↓←↑△→↓◎↑
                 → crouch ↓ Backside-360 ↑
                 → crouch Inverted-Backside-360

(28) Linear Combinations (1/2)

28.1. & 28.2.

𝕐 𝕄 𝔽	ko-no-so
𝕋 𝕍 𝕏𝕏 𝔽	a-mi-ni-so
𝕏 𝕍 𝕋	pa-i-to
𝕍 𝕏 𝔽	tu-ri-so
𝕏 𝕏 𝕏𝕏 𝕋	ku-do-ni-a
𝕋 𝕏 𝔼 𝕄	a-pa-ta-wa
𝕐 𝕍 𝕋	ru-ki-to
𝔽 𝔼 𝕄	u-ta-no
𝕏 𝕄 𝕏 𝕐	ku-pi-ri-jo
𝕍 𝕏𝕏 ☐	tu-ni-ja

135

(28) Linear Combinations (2/2)

28.3.

〒	a	〰	no
〒	do	‡	pa
Ⅴ	i	𝍫	pi
▯	ja	𝍨	ri
？	jo	↑	ru
⊽	ki	🇫	so
𝍠	ko	匚	ta
⅄	ku	〒	to
⅁	mi	♡	tu
ⅩⅩ	ni	𝍬	u
		⊓	wa

28.4.

𝍠 ⊓	'girl'	ko-wa
‡ 匚	'all'	pa-ta
〒 🇫	'this'	to-so
⅄ ⅁ 〰	'Cumin'	ku-mi-no
⅟ 〰	'linen'	ri-no

(29) Easy Pieces (1/1)

In Bulgarian, the adjectives agree in number with the nouns they modify. Thus, a noun in plural is accompanied by an adjective in plural, and a noun in singular is accompanied by an adjective in singular.

The formation of the plural of the nouns is complex and cannot be deduced from the data presented in this problem. The specific noun plural form is not relevant to the formation of the plural of the adjective which accompanies it.

29.1. The problem presents only a partial picture of the formation of the plural of the adjectives. The three rules could be formulated in various ways, essentially equivalent to the following:

a. If the singular ends in –ęn (stressed), then just add –i: **červęn** : **červęni**.
b. If the adjective indicates from what matter the noun is made, then just add –i: **kǫsten** : **kǫsteni**.
c. In all other cases, drop the final e and add –i: **gnęven** : **gnęvni**.

29.2. The rule which is used in the formation of each adjective is written in parenthesis next to it.

19	**obiknovęni** (a) procedụri	ordinary procedures
20	**lęsni** (c) urǫci	easy lessons
21	**rịbni** (c) restorạnti	fish restaurants
22	**kǫstni** (c) zabolyạvaniya	bone diseases
23	**lęneni** (b) čaršạfi	linen sheets

(30) Hypo-Hmong-driac (1/1)

To solve this problem, it is important to realize that both collections of words can be seen as networks, where words are connected by hyponymy relationships, and that these two networks must have equivalent shapes. However, since "matching up" a whole network (or "graph") of this kind with another is difficult even for a computer, solving this problem requires noting that the graphs are largely composed of smaller graphs with a tree-like shape. These are much simpler to deal with.

28	be lost	26	lose money ("silver")
17	beef	2	lungs
6	beverage	8	money
15	Bovine livestock	14	small, non-bovine livestock
13	chicken (the animal)	11	pig (the animal)
10	dog (the animal)	22	poetic genre ("money-language")
12	filthy animals; filth	7	silver
23	filthy language	30	suffer from a headache ("brain-ache")
18	flesh; meat	29	suffer from grief ("liver-ache")
32	hurt	31	suffer from lung disease ("lung-ache")
3	internal organs; soul	4	water
24	language	21	water-buffalo liver
1	liver (the organ)	9	wealth
16	livestock	5	whisky
25	lose heart ("liver"); lose one's wits; panic	20	young female
27	lose life to water; drown	19	young sow

For example, you might observe that there are exactly two components of the graph where three words are hyponyms of a single word (like a tree with three branches) for both the Hmong and English collections. This allows you to infer that 25-28 and 29-32 must be either 'be lost' and the 'lose' words or 'hurt' and the 'suffer' words. You can determine how to match them by noting that only one of the roots in the Hmong words does not occur elsewhere (*hlwb*) and that only one of the English meanings does not occur elsewhere ('brain'). This suggests that 29-32 must be the 'hurt/suffer' group, and 25-28 must be the 'lost/lose' group. Furthermore, since *sab* occurs in both of these groups, and since 'liver' occurs in both groups, *sab* must be 'liver', *sab-twm* must be 'water-buffalo liver' and *twm* must mean 'water buffalo'.

This will lead you to the livestock tree in 12-16 and the realization that Hmong compounds are of at least two types. In one type, the meaning of the whole is the meaning of the first part modified by the second part (as in *sab-twm*). In the second type, the meaning of the whole is a general category including the meaning of both parts (that is, both parts are hyponyms of the whole). Knowing that *twm* is 'water buffalo' should allow you to guess that *nyuj-twm* is 'bovine livestock', since 'water buffalo' is a hyponym of only 'livestock' and 'bovine livestock', 'bovine livestock' is a hyponymn of 'livestock', and *nyuj-twm* is a hyponym of *qab-npua-nyuj-twm*. We can now see that 3, 6, 9, and 12 are all compounds of the second type, and reason from what is known about their parts that 3 and 6 must be 'internal organs; soul' and 'beverage'. We see that 12 must be 'filthy animals; filth', since it occurs embedded inside of a type one compound that can only mean 'filthy language' (23). Therefore, 14 must be 'small, non-bovine livestock'.

By applying similar logic to the remaining cases, you will arrive at the answer given above.

(31) The Gerbil Arrived (1/1)

Word order:

* SOV (subject-object-verb) — in case the subject is a pronoun.
* OSV (object-subject-verb) — in case the subject is not a pronoun.

Pronouns:

* ŋinda = you
* ŋađa = I

Definite articles:

* bayi, placed before subjects of intransitive verbs and objects of transitive verbs.
* baŋgul, placed before subjects of transitive verbs.

The suffix -ŋgu is placed on the subject of transitive verbs when the subject is not a pronoun.

31.1. The boy returned.
The kangaroo waked the man.
You saw the kangaroo.

31.2. ŋinda ñinañu
ŋađa bayi yuṛi ñiman.
bayi yaṛa baŋgul ŋumaŋgu walmbin.

(32) Yak, Du, Dray (1/4)

This is a very complex and tricky problem. One needs to start with the most obvious alignments and guesses, and then use logic to complete the rest.

1. Build a table going west to east (easier than east to west, since English is near the western end).

2. Include the known words in the table, including the words in English.

3. Identify global patterns – e.g., words for 5 start with a "P", words for 9 start with an "N", group words by other similar initial and final consonant clusters, etc. Vowel matches get a lower priority.

4. Realize that Yiddish and German are very close matches (as far as numbers are concerned).

5. One can then realize that NAYN-EYNS in Yiddish is 9-1, so F=8.

6. Then get as many other matches as possible, e.g., Lithuanian 3, 4, 5, 6, 7, 8 (which yields H=8-5=3), Albanian 3, 4, Irish 3, 4, 8, 9, Farsi 4, 5, 6 (SHEST is similar to ŠEŠI in Lithuanian).

7. Get some harder matches such as Lithuanian 10, Irish 1, 2, 5, 6, 7, 10, Albanian 9, Farsi 8, 9, Farsi 3 (SE cannot be 10 at this time and is unlikely to be 2, so it must be 3).

8. From the title of the problem, YAK = 1, DU = 2.

9. Now one can link to Nepali, EK from YAK.

10. We can now compute D=6-5=1 and C=8-3=5.

11. A few others can be filled in – e.g. Albanian 1, 5, 6, 10, therefore B=10-6=4, from there Nepali 2.

	Indo-European									Dravidian	
	Irish	**German**	**Yiddish**	**Latin**	**Alb**	**AncGrk**	**Lith**	**Farsi**	**Nepali**	**Pengo**	**Kuvi**
1	AON	EINS	EYNS	UNUS	NJË	EN		YAK	EK		
2	DÓ	ZWEI	TSVEY	DUO		DUO	DU		DUI		
3	TRÍ	DREI	DRAY	TRES	TRE	TRIA	TRYS	SE			
4	CEATHAIR	VIER	FIR	QUATTUOR	KATËR	TETTARA	KETURI	CHAHAR			
5	CÚIG	FÜNF	FINF	QUINQUE	PESË	PENTE	PENKI	PANJ	PANCH	PÃC	PA:SA
6	SÉ	SECHS	ZEKS	SEX	GJASHTË	HEX	ŠEŠI	SHESH			
7	SEACHT	SIEBEN	ZIBN	SEPTEM		HEPTA	SEPTYNI				
8	OCHT	ACHT	AKHT	OCTO		OCTO	AŠTUONI	HASHT			
9	NAOI	NEUN	NAYN	NOVEM	NËNTË	ENNEA		NOH	NAU	NOV	NO:
10	DEICH	ZEHN	TSEN	DECEM	DHJETË	DECA	DEŠIMT				

12. Status so far – we have most of the 8 westernmost languages completed. Some numbers will not need to be matched, e.g., Farsi 2, 10 and Lithuanian 1, 9.
Now starts the harder part.

13. Nepali and Pengo are closely aligned. It follows that EK and DUI must match RO and RI in some order.

14. Kuvi's RINDI must match RI, so RINDI is either 1 or 2.

15. So, far we have accounted for the differences of 1, 3, 4, 5, 8. Therefore the other three missing differences must be three among 2, 6, 7, 9. Let's start with 7 and 9 (being longer, they can possibly match only a handful of number pairs).

16. There are three possible cases: we have both a 7 and 9 (case A), we only have a 9 (case B), or we only have a 7 (case C).

17. Let's consider case A first. The only way to get a 9 is in Kuvi (A:TA=10, RINDI=1). Then the only way left to form a 7 is in either Pengo or Nepali to get a 10-3. However, this implies that DAS and AT must both match the same number whereas we expected that they would be the same in both languages. This is not compatible with the observations that the numbers above 3 are (nearly) identical in both languages. So, case A is not possible.

18. Case B is when we have a 9 but no 7 (in other words, the remaining three differences are 2, 6, 9). Again, we'd need to have Kuvi A:TA - RINDI = 10-1 =9. Therefore the 6 will be in either Pengo or Nepali as a 10-4. However, this again implies that DAS and AT must match the same numeral in the two languages which is not allowed. Therefore, case B is also not possible.

19. This leaves us with case C. The remaining differences are therefore 2, 6, and 7. There are now three possibilities for the 7. These are Case X (Nepali 10-3), Case Y (Kuvi 8-1), and Case Z (Pengo 10-3). All others are inconsistent with the data so far.

20. Let's now consider case X. The 6 must now be in Pengo (10-4) but this again leads to a mismatch for DAS. So, case X is not possible.

21. Case Y now. There are two possible solutions for the 6. (Pengo 10-4) is ok but leads to no possible answers for a 2 in Nepali. Conversely, (Nepali 10-4) is ok but leads to no possible answers for a 2 in Pengo. Therefore case Y is also not possible.

22. Now case Z. There are 4 possibilities for Kuvi (3-1, case J), (4-2, case K), (7-1, case L), and (8-2, case M). Of these, case J leads to a conflict for A:TA, case K leads to no possible match for Nepali, and case L leads to no match in the main equation.

23. Case L (Pengo 10-3, Kuvi 8-2, and Nepali 6-4) is the only one that works so far. We can now fill Nepali 4 and 6, Pengo 3 and 10, and Kuvi 2 and 8. We have solved the problem. From now on, we can just play and fill out a few more cells.

24. From known alignments from before we can now add Nepali 3, 8, 10, followed by Pengo 1, 2, 8, and Kuvi 10.

25. The table so far:

	Nepali	Pengo	Kuvi
1	EK	RO	
2	DUI	RI	RINDI
3	TIN	TIN	
4	CHA:R		
5	PA:NCH	PÃC	PA:SA
6	CHA		
7			
8	A:T	AT	A:TA
9	NAU	NOV	NO:
10	DAS	DAS	DOS

141

(32) Yak, Du, Dray (3/4)

25. We can now try and solve:

$$(PA{:}SA \times SA{:}RI) + (NO{:} \times A{:}TA) = (PA{:}SA \times DOS) + (SO{:} \times SA{:}TA)$$

$$(5 \times SA{:}RI) + (9 \times 8) = (5 \times 10) + (SO{:} \times SA{:}TA)$$

26. The allowable values for the missing SA:RI, SO:, SA:TA are among 1, 3, 4, 6, 7. The only combination that works is SA:RI=4 and SO: x SA:TA=42. However, from the SA:T/SA:TA alignment (in Nepali/Pengo), it follows that SA:TA must be 7. Therefore SO:=6.

27. Final table (except for Kuvi 1 and 3, which were never given in the problem – the missing numbers there are RONDI=1 and TI:NI=3).

					Indo-European						Dravidian	
	Irish	**German**	**Yiddish**	**Latin**	**Alb**	**AncGrk**	**Lith**	**Farsi**	**Nepali**	**Pengo**	**Kuvi**
1	AON	EINS	EYNS	UNUS	NJË	EN	VIENAS	YAK	EK	RO	RONDI
2	DÓ	ZWEI	TSVEY	DUO	Dy	DUO	DU	DO	DUI	RI	RINDI
3	TRÍ	DREI	DRAY	TRES	TRE	TRIA	TRYS	SE	TIN	TIN	TI:NI
4	CEATHAIR	VIER	FIR	QUATTUOR	KATËR	TETTARA	KETURI	CHAHAR	CHA:R	CAR	SARI
5	CÚIG	FÜNF	FINF	QUINQUE	PESË	PENTE	PENKI	PANJ	PA:NCH	PÃC	PA:SA
6	SÉ	SECHS	ZEKS	SEX	GJASHTË	HEX	ŠEŠI	SHESH	CHA	CO	SO:
7	SEACHT	SIEBEN	ZIBN	SEPTEM	SHTATË	HEPTA	SEPTYNI	HAFT	SA:T	SAT	SA:TA
8	OCHT	ACHT	AKHT	OCTO	TETË	OCTO	AŠTUONI	HASHT	A:T	AT	A:TA
9	NAOI	NEUN	NAYN	NOVEM	NËNTË	ENNEA	DEVYNI	NOH	NAU	NOV	NO:
10	DEICH	ZEHN	TSEN	DECEM	DHJETË	DECA	DEŠIMT	Dah	DAS	DAS	DOS

28. Note that the numbers RO and RI in Pengo come from Proto-Dravidian. The rest are Indo-European.

29. There are many other ways to solve this puzzle. They involve various mixtures of similarity guessing and logic. Backtracking is important – if a particular guess is invalid, one may have to go back and replace it.

30. Reference: http://www.zompist.com/euro.htm

(32) Yak, Du, Dray (4/4)

32.1.

1	2	3	4	5	6	7	8	9
D	E	H	B	C	A	G	F	_

Intermediate data:

A. **Kuvi** 8-2=6
B. **Albanian** 10-6=4
C. **Farsi** 8-3=5
D. **Irish** 6-5=1
E. **Nepali** 6-4=2
F. **Yiddish** 9-1=8
G. **Pengo** 10-3=7
H. **Lithuanian** 8-5=3

$(5 \times 4)+(9 \times 8)=(5 \times 10)+(6 \times 7)$

32.2. A number of "key insights" are listed below.

- closer connections among neighboring languages
- consonants more likely to be preserved
- pronunciation may not match spelling
- specific phonological changes, e.g., s—sh, c—p
- specific patterns for numerals, e.g., **9** starts with N, **4** has T+R in the middle
- use of the title of the problem
- use of the equation
- use of the constraints imposed by the subtractions
- the form for the number **1** changes the most

(33) Orwellspeak (1/4)

33.1. Here is the revised grammar. The changes are relatively small.

Sentence → PosNounPhrase + Verb + NegNounPhrase
Sentence → NegNounPhrase + Verb + PosNounPhrase

PosNounPhrase → PosAdjective + Noun
PosNounPhrase → PosAdjective + PosNounPhrase
NegNounPhrase → NegAdjective + Noun
NegNounPhrase → NegAdjective + NegNounPhrase

Noun → people
Verb → love
PosAdjective → good
PosAdjective → charming
PosAdjective → happy
NegAdjective → bad
NegAdjective → obnoxious
NegAdjective → unhappy

Notice that in this grammar, a single Noun does not qualify as a PosNounPhrase or NegNounPhrase. This ensures that the false statement "people love good people" is ungrammatical, since "people" is not a NegNounPhrase.

33.2. Could it help to list 1-word bad phrases? No. You can't list any of the 8 vocabulary words without ruling out some legal sentences. (And there is no point in listing words outside that vocabulary, since they will have no effect, and you were asked to keep your list as short as possible.)

How about 2-word bad phrases? There are 25 types of 2-word phrases: the first word can be from any of the 5 categories {START, Noun, Verb, PosAdjective, NegAdjective}, and the second word can be from any of the categories {Noun, Verb, PosAdjective, NegAdjective, END}. Of these 25 types, the following 15 types can never appear in a legal sentence, so we list them as bad phrases:

    START Noun (1)
    START Verb (1)
    START END (1)

    Noun Noun (1)
    Noun PosA (3)
    Noun NegA (3)

    Verb Noun (1)

Verb Verb (1)
Verb END (1)

PosA Verb (3)
PosA NegA (9)
PosA END (3)

NegA Verb (3)
NegA PosA (9)
NegA END (3)

The *remaining* 10 types are depicted by the 10 arrows in this graph:

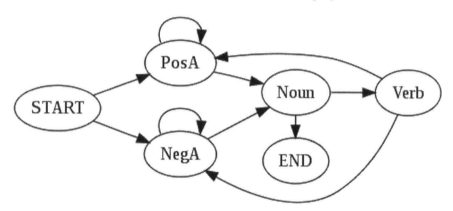

By allowing only those 10 types of 2-word phrases, the device so far allows any sentence that corresponds to a path in the graph. Now, where does that leave us? As you can see, this already ensures that

- START must be followed by one or more Adjectives of the same type, and then a Noun. In other words, START must be followed by a PosNounPhrase or NegNounPhrase.
- Such a PosNounPhrase or NegNounPhrase may be followed by END, or else may be followed by a Verb and another PosNounPhrase or NegNounPhrase.

However, this still permits illegal utterances like

A1. good people (not a sentence)
B1. good people love good people (not true)
C1. good people love bad people love good people (not a sentence)

and similarly

A2. good charming people
B2. good charming people love good charming people
C2. good charming people love bad obnoxious people love good charming people

(33) Orwellspeak (3/4)

We can get rid of some of the A sentences with the 4-word bad phrases

> START PosA Noun END (3)
> START NegA Noun END (3)

This is only able to get rid of the shortest A utterances, such as A1. We would need longer bad phrases to get rid of A2, since every 4-word subsequence of A2 can be part of a legal sentence. No finite list of bad phrases can get rid of all the A utterances—even with an upgraded device that allowed 1000-word bad phrases, we would not be able to censor extremely long A utterances.

Similarly, we can get rid of some of the C sentences with the 4-word bad phrases

> Verb PosA Noun Verb (3)
> Verb NegA Noun Verb (3)

Again, this is only able to get rid of the shortest C utterances, such as C1. We would need longer bad phrases to get rid of C2, and no finite list could get rid of all the C utterances.

However, we can get rid of **all** of the B utterances with only the 4-word bad phrases

> PosA Noun Verb PosA (9)
> NegA Noun Verb NegA (9)

These require successive noun phrases to be of opposite polarity. They work on noun phrases of **any** length by requiring the first phrase's last adjective to oppose the second phrase's first adjective. For example, we are able to censor B2. because it contains "… charming people love good …"

The total number of bad phrases above is 73.

33.3. Yes. It fails to censor A2 and C2 above.

33.4. A single 1-word bad phrase will satisfy the government's stated needs by censoring everything:
START
Or they could use
END

(Or if the device can allow 0-word bad phrases, then the single 0-word phrase "" will also censor everything, as it is contained in any utterance; think about it!)

You may be interested in some connections to computational linguistics:

(33) Orwellspeak (4/4)

- Part 1 asked you to write a tiny context-free grammar. It is possible to write large context-free grammars that describe a great deal of English or another language. Although the "Opposites Attract" setting was whimsical, you could use similar techniques to ensure that plural noun phrases are not the subjects of singular verbs, and—for many languages—that plural noun phrases only contain plural adjectives.

- Part 2 asked you to approximate the context-free grammar by what is called a 3rd-order Markov model, meaning that the model's opinion of the legality or probability of each word depends solely on the previous 3 words. (That is, the model only considers 4-word phrases.) The graph shown partway through the solution depicts a 1st-order Markov model (which considered only 2-word phrases).

- Part 3 showed that the Markov model was only an approximation of the context-free grammar—it did not define exactly the same set of legal sentences. The solution further noted that **no** nth-order Markov model could exactly match this context-free grammar, not even for every large n.

- If you know about regular expressions, you may have noticed that the following regular expression **would** be equivalent to the context-free grammar, hence would do a perfect job of censorship.

  START (((PosA)+ Noun Verb (NegA)+ Noun)
  | ((NegA)+ Noun Verb (PosA)+ Noun)) END

- Regular expressions or regular grammars are equivalent to finite-state machines. They are not as powerful as context-free grammars in general, but they are powerful enough to match the "Opposites Attract" grammar. They are essentially equivalent to hidden Markov models, an important generalization of Markov models.

- Parts 3 and 4 together were intended to make you think about how to measure errors. In general, a system that tries to identify bad sentences (or bad poetry or email spam or interesting news stories) may make two kinds of errors: it may identify too many things or too few. Both kinds of errors are bad, and there is a tradeoff: you can generally reduce one kind at the expense of the other kind. The original requirement in part 2 was to completely avoid the first type of error (i.e., never censor good stuff) while simultaneously trying to avoid the second type of error (censor as much bad stuff as possible). But the revised requirement in part 4 considered only the second type of error, giving the vendor an incentive to design a dumb system that did horribly on the first type of error. You might conclude that when evaluating a vendor's system or setting requirements for it, you should pay attention to both kinds of error.

(34) Anishinaabemowin (1/1)

34.1.

Minnesota Ojibwe	Nishnaabemwin	English
amik	mik	beaver
mitig	mtig	tree
okosimān	kosmān	pumpkin
makizinan	mkiznan	moccasins
niwābamigonān	nwābmignān	he or she sees us
makwa	mkwa	bear
adōpowin	dōpwin	table

34.2.

Minnesota Ojibwe	Nishnaabemwin	English
mōz	mōz	moose
ginebig	gnebig	snake
manidō	mnidō	Manitou, spirit
mitigwāb	mtigwāb	bow
opwāgan	pwāgan	pipe

34.3.

Minnesota Ojibwe	Nishnaabemwin	English
jīmān	jīmān	canoe
ēsibanag	ēsbanag	raccoons
aninātig	ninātig	maple tree
anishinābēmowin	nishnābēmwin	Indian language
gichi-mōkomān	gchi-mōkmān	American
mīgwan	mīgwan	feather
gwīwizens	gwīwzens	boy
nimishōmis	nmishōmis	my grandfather

Correct final algorithms will have the results that every odd vowel deletes, counting from the left, except for the final vowel in a word, and except for long vowels, which "restart" the counting process anew with the next vowel.

(35) Handwriting Recognition (1/1)

35.1. My alarm clock did not wake me up this morning.

35.2. (Many possible answers here—this is only one possibility). You could compare the combinations of words to a huge corpus of English, say blogs on the internet, and see which words occur together and which don't. For example, you would get a lot of hits on "my alarm clock" but few, if any, on "lie charm code", "my solemn circle", "my charm chute", "bye beam block", etc. The program would first take each word in the first column and combine it with each word in the second column and search the corpus to determine which combinations are most likely. Then, it would take the most likely two-word combinations (probably all those starting with "my"), and combine them with each word in the third column to form three-word combinations, and search the corpus for those. Then, the most likely three-word combinations would be combined with each possible fourth word to form four-word combinations, etc., until the one most likely 10-word combination is determined.

(36) Hawaiian (1/1)

36.1. i. I have no elder brothers (Keone/male speaking).
ii. I have no elder sisters (Mele/female speaking).

36.2. I have no sisters (Keone speaking).

36.3. <u>Keone has one brother.</u> — In Hawaiian, the word for the brother of a boy and a sister of a girl are the same and they are always distinguished according to age—younger or older. Thus, there is no way to say "Keone has one brother" in Hawaiian without saying whether the brother is younger or older.

<u>Mele has one younger brother.</u> — The words for brother of a girl and sister of a boy are not distinguished by age. So, you could easily say "Mele has one brother," but not "Mele has one younger brother," given the words available in this problem.

(37) Maasai (1/1)

1. G

2. H

3. E

4. F

5. I

6. D

7. J

8. B

9. A

10. C

(38) Getting the Hang of Hangul (1/2)

38.1. A-17 B-7 C-14 D-5 E-13 F-12 G-16 H-2
I-1 J-3 K-11 L-10 M-8 N-6 O-15 P-4 Q-9

Method: Each symbol represents a syllable, separated by a hyphen in the transcription. Only one word has three syllables: L=10, and once you know that 자 = JA, you can look for the other words that have this syllable (A,B,F) and match them with 7,12,17. And/or you can look at the one-syllable words E and K and match them with 11 and 13. To do either of these tasks, you have to realize that each individual symbol can be further broken down into its component parts. So in 자 = JA, ㅈ is the J, and ㅏ is the A. Some of the syllables involve three sounds, such as 찬 = CHAN, where we have the same symbol for A, with ㅊ for CH top left and ㄴ for N underneath. When a syllable begins with a vowel, there is a dummy consonant that looks like an O, e.g., 오 = AW. But the same symbol, when it appears at the end of a syllable, is used for NG, e.g., 창 = CHANG

The consonants represented in the data are:
J, N, G, T, M, B, S, P, CH, L, NG, H, D

The vowels are:
A, O, U, I, AW, OO

38.2. a. jag-un (small) = 작은

   b. nawng-jang (field) = 농장

   c. na-moo (tree) = 나무

   d. gaw-mab-sub-ni-da (thank you) = 고맙습니다

The problem for this question is that some of the syllables have not been seen in the data, so you have to figure out how to compose them from the parts. For example, for JAG, we have seen JA = 자 and TAG = 탁, etc.

In a and b, there is no clear indication from the data whether to write the three parts of the symbol vertically or in a triangle, so either layout is allowable, although the ones shown here are the correct ones.

38.3. a. 산 (mountain) = SAN

   b. 들반 (field) = DUL-BAN

   c. 물고기 (fish) = MOOL-GAW-GI

(38) Getting the Hang of Hangul (2/2)

Again, some of the symbols have not been seen in the data, so you have to figure out how to decompose them.

38.4. **a.** 가벼운 (light) = GA-BYO-OON

b. 이때 (now) = I-DDIO or I-DDAI

c. 바꾸다 (to change) = BA-GGOO-DA

d. 가운데 (in the middle) = GA-OON-DOI

e. 안녕히계세요 (goodbye) = AN-NYONG-HI-GYOI-SOI-YAW

The new data introduces a new consonant K ㅋ, and three new devices: double consonants (the symbol is just repeated, e.g., ㅃ BB), diphthongs (two vowel sounds combined, e.g., ㅔ OI), and new derived vowel symbols YOO and YO. You should notice the relationship between OO and YOO (OO = ㅜ, YOO ㅠ) and similarly for O and YO (ㅓ,) and make the generalization about the double stroke.

You may also have noticed a relationship between certain consonant pairs, ㅈ ㅊ J/CH, ㅂ ㅍ B/P, ㄷ ㅌ D/T which is not coincidental.

The ㅐ symbol in 4b is actually AI, but from the data given you can't tell whether it is ㅏ + ㅣ (AI) or ㅣ + ㅓ (IO).

38.5. **a.** Han-goog (Korea) = 한국

b. Pyong-yang (capital of North Korea) = 평 양

c. Pag Ji Song (a Korean footballer (soccer player): [pag] is usually written Park) = 팍지승

d. A-il-lion-du (Ireland) = 아일랜드

(39) Scrabble® (1/1)

39.1. *H, I, S, T,* and *U* are the only letters whose tile count either increases or decreases by more than one.

39.2. It explains *H, S, T,* and *U*. *H, S,* and *T* are all more common in this list even than their overall token frequency, which is already higher than their Scrabble® frequency. *U* does not appear in any of the most common words, so its underrepresentation in overall token frequency is also accounted for. The list does not explain the letter *I*, however. *I* is less common in overall token frequency than its Scrabble® frequency would suggest, but it is more common in the most frequent twenty words.

39.3. The frequencies of the words in the list explain *H* and *T* even better, because they both occur in *the*. It continues to explain *U*, which continues to be absent. The data no longer explains *S* as well, because *S* does not occur in the most frequent of these words. *I*, however, is now better explained. It is underrepresented in the top seven words (those more frequent than one percent, comprising 21% of all tokens) among vowels. *E* occurs only once, but in the most common (by far) word. *A* and *O* both occur twice in the rest of the top five. On the other hand, *I* only occurs in *in*. Therefore, this new data do help explain why *I* might have about the same number of Scrabble® tiles as *A* and *O*, though it has a smaller corpus frequency.

(40) Walrus (1/1)

The letter *ß* (pronounced es-tsett) exists only in the German language. It is written to render the voiceless sound [s], as well as the letter combination *ss*. Before the reform, the rules for using either variant were rather complex and inconsistent. The reform offers a simpler rule: after a long vowel or diphthong, one writes *ß*, as long as no other consonant follows in the word stem (the latter part is not reflected in the problem).

The problem can be solved without using any knowledge of German, if one compares the German words to their English cognates. We can see that in each syllable which contains the *ß*, English has two vowel letters: *barfuß – barefoot*, *groß – great*, *Soße – sauce*, *Straße – street*, *süß – sweet*. This may be an indication of the fact that the joint ancestor of German and English had a long vowel in this position. The traditional German orthography does not show the length of the vowel in any way, but we may suppose that the long/short distinction still exists in the language. Then, it would be reasonable to assume that according to the new orthography, the length of the vowel in the syllable ending by the [s] sound is reflected by the use of *ß* or *ss*.

40.1.

Baß	Bass	bass
Biß	Biss	bit
Floß	Floß	float
Fußball	Fußball	football
Geißhirt	Geißhirt	goatherd
grüß	grüß	greet
schieß	schieß	shoot
Schuß	Schuss	shot
Schweiß	Schweiß	sweat

40.2. The new orthography apparently makes it easier to read some German words for foreigners, who otherwise would not know whether to pronounce the vowel in a given word short or long.

(41) Sentence Endings (1/1)

41.1. The rule is good enough to find all sentences in the text. The sentences are:

The Bank of New York ADR Index, which tracks depositary receipts traded on major U.S. stock exchanges, gained 1.3% to 183.32 points in recent session.

The index lost 4.63 from the beginning of July.

American Depository Receipts are dollar-denominated securities that are traded in the U.S. but represent ownership of shares in a non-U.S. company.

41.2. & 41.3. The rule would fail in text like this:

How funny! She didn't know where to go.

This sentence (and many others) use other characters than full stop to mark an end of sentence. The amended rule would keep a list of characters that are candidates of being sentence separators, such as '?' and '!'. The best way to find all sentence separators would be to go through real text and see what is actually used to end sentences.

The rule would also fail here:

I saw Mr. Smith.

The problem is that names appear in uppercase. The system would need to keep a list of abbreviations that are likely to be followed by names, such as titles, and ideally to identify names. But there are no fool-proof rules to solve this problem, because sometimes the abbreviation is ambiguous (e.g., *St. Michael* vs. *High St.* or even *Dr. Fox* vs. *Fox Dr.*)

Another problematic case is when there are quotation marks. Some editing house rules recommend to place the closing quotation mark after punctuation. Also, the first word of a sentence could begin with an opening quotation mark. The rule would need to accommodate all these cases.

Mary was `volunteered.' But she wasn't happy about it.

Peter arrived. `It's so funny', he thought.

(42) Counting in Etruscan (1/1)

42.1.

	thu	
	I	
sa	max	ci
I	5	3
	huth	
	6	
	zal	
	2	

42.2. There are two possible solutions.

	thu	
	i	
sa	max	ci
urti	caius	est
	huth	
	volote	
	zal	
	va	

	thu	
	volote	
sa	max	ci
est	caius	va
	huth	
	urti	
	zal	
	i	

42.3. For the first solution above: The number of letters in each word symbolizes the number.
For the second solution above: The order of the words in the proverb corresponds
to the number, e.g., first word = 1, last word = 6.

(43) Tamil 1 (1/1)

43.1. All geminates (doubled consonants) appear intervocalically. We have no examples of geminate fricatives, and all voiced fricatives appear intervocalically, except for <v>, which appears at the beginning of "viral", "vanda:y".

Voiced plosives only appear before nasals, which always match their place of articulation, except for <ḍ>, which also appears intervocalically in 4. Voiceless plosives do not appear intervocalically, except <ḍ> in 4.

<š> appears in the same conditions as voiced fricatives, and <č> appears in the same conditions as voiceless plosives.. <ɻ> only appears intervocalically or at the end of a word

Syllable structure is generally (N)C(:)V(:), meaning optionally a nasal onset if the following consonant is a plosive or affricate, a possibly geminate consonant, and a possibly long vowel. However, the final syllable in a word may have a coda of <m, n, l, y ḷ, ɻ, i>. Also, the first syllable in a word need not have a consonantal onset, and it may not contain the optional nasal or a geminate consonant.

<ñ, ŋ> only appear as a nasal onset to syllables containing voiced consonants of their place of articulation.

43.2. Vowels:

/a/, /e/, /i/, /u/, /o/

/ɨ/ — only appears in the last syllable or in a syllable adjacent to one containing /ɨ/

/a:/, /e:/, /o:/, /i:/, /u:/

[NB: In the traditional analysis of Tamil, ɨ is considered an allophone of /u/ in non-initial syllables. However, this is not completely clear from the given data.]

Plosives/Affricates — listed allophones occur intervocalically and after a nasal, respectively:

/p/ - [β], [b]   /t/ - [.], [d]   /č/ - [š], [ǰ]   /ṭ/ - [ḍ], [ḍ]   /k/ - [ɣ], [g]

Nasals

/m/, /n/, /ṇ/, /N/ — archiphoneme; only occurs before a plosive/affricate and assimilates to its POA ([ñ, ŋ] are not phonemic).

Approximants/Trills

/v/, /l/, /y/, /r/, /ɻ/

Solution contributed by Morris Alper

(44) The Fall of Yers (1/1)

44.1. Here is the full table.

OCS	Bulgarian	Russian	English Meaning
beroN	bera	beru	*I gather/I take*
kralь	kral	korol'	*king*
krъvь	krăv	krov'	*blood*
zoNbъ	zăb	zub	*tooth*

44.2. These were probably vowels:

Firstly, a word like "dьnьsь" would be difficult to pronounce without vowels, though syllabic consonant nuclei are possible.

Secondly, they have shifted into vowels in some positions in Bulgarian and Russian, and never independent consonants. The only non-vowel reflex of these sounds is the palatalization in Russian (represented by an apostrophe), and even this is easily explainable if /ь/ was at some point a front vowel.

Finally, their ellipsis word-finally is consistent with the behavior of vowels, while it is less common diachronically for consonants.

(45) Eat Your Words! (1/1)

45.1. The translations are shown below.

English	Arabic Equivalent
a big strawberry	fraizāya kbīra
the big apricot	al-mi<u>sh</u>mi<u>sh</u>i l-əkbīri
some biscuity cake	<u>sh</u>wayyit ka^ck
a lot of sugar	sukkar əktīr əktīr
a pepper	filəfli [analogy "radish"]
beef	laHm baqar à laHəm baqar

There is no evidence for the final "a" in the data. The best one can get from the data is "kbīri".

45.2. Where there is a sequence of three consonants/to break up a sequence of three consonants

45.3. Where there is a sequence of three consonants, 'ə' is inserted/appears/comes after the first one (CCC > CəCC)

45.4. 'ə' is added after 'l' to avoid a sequence of 3 consonants/this variant avoids a sequence of 3 consonants, AND al > l OR al- is only allowed on the first word (of a phrase). 39 can be used as a model.

45.5. The completed table is shown below.

'cucumber'	Example	Explanation
xyār	23	basic word/ stem/ citation form/generic term
xyāra	15	-a added to mean 'a' / 'a cucumber'/specific/particular cucumber
əxyār	34	'ə' is inserted to avoid 3 consonants (txy > təxy)
l-əxyār	39	'l' marks 'the', 'ə' is inserted to avoid 3 consonants (lxy >ləxy)

(46) Noun-Noun Compounds (1/1)

Answers will vary. Here are a few examples:

- Sunday school = School ON Sunday

- Shoebox = Box FOR shoes

- Cherry tomato = Tomato LIKE cherry

- Chess tournament = Tournament IN chess

- Panama hat = Hat FROM Panama

- Cup holder = Holder OF cup **or** Holder FOR cup

- Gunmen = Men WITH guns

- War story = Story ABOUT war

- Airport food = Food AT airport

(47) A Killer Puzzle (1/1)

47.1. Джон убил Сэма.

47.2. Мэри убила Джона.

47.3. Сэм убил Мэри.

(48) It's All Greek to Me (1/1)

48.1. The definitions are as follows.

- Barology — the science of weight or gravity
- Bibliophobia — a fear of books
- Cardialgia — pain in the heart region (i.e., heartburn)
- Dromomania — a passion for wandering, traveling, running
- Gynophilia — the love of women
- Hippophobia — a fear of horses
- Logophobia — a fear of words
- Misandry — hatred of males
- Misanthropy — hatred of humankind
- Misogamy — hatred of marriage
- Monandry — the practice or condition of having one husband at a time; (of a female animal) the condition of having one mate at a time.
- Monoglottism — the condition of being able to speak only a single language
- Mystagogue — someone who instructs others before initiation into religious mysteries or before participation in the sacraments; a person whose teachings are said to be founded on mystical revelations
- Pedagogue — a schoolteacher
- Philanthropism — an affection for mankind, especially as manifested in the devotion of work or wealth to persons or socially useful purposes; the activity of revealing this affection

48.2. More definitions.

- Antinomy — opposition between one law, principle, rule, etc., and another; a contradiction between two statements, both apparently obtained by correct reasoning
- Apatheist — a person who may accept the existence of a god, but who does not care about that god's existence.
- Axiology — the branch of philosophy dealing with values, as those of ethics, aesthetics, or religion
- Dactyloscopy — a method of studying fingerprints to establish identification
- Enneagon — a polygon having nine angle and nine sides (synonym: nonagon)
- Oology — the branch of ornithology (the branch of zoology that deals with birds) that studies birds' eggs
- Paraskevidekatriaphobia — a fear of Friday the 13th
- Philadelphia — the city of brotherly love
- Phytology — the study of plants (synonym: botany)
- Triskaidekaphobia — a fear concerning the number 13

Definitions provided by Dictionary.com, Wiktionary, and The Free Dictionary by Farlex.

(49) Zoque (1/1)

49.1.

Zoque	English	Zoque	English
pən	*man*	hiʔŋ	*with*
taʔm	*plural/more than one*	yomo	*woman*
kəsi	*on*	ʔune	*small/little/child*
kotoya	*for*	maŋ	*go*
keʔt	*also*	min	*come*
šeh	*like/as*	u	*past (on verb)*
tih	*just/only*	pa	*present (on verb)*
kahši	*hen*	teʔ	*the*

49.2.

English	Zoque
The child came.	Minu teʔ ʔune.
The girl also went.	Maŋkeʔtu teʔ yomoʔune.
with children	ʔunehiʔŋtaʔm
for women	yomokotoyataʔm

49.3.

Zoque	English
maŋutih teʔ yomoʔune	*The girl just/only went.*
yomotihtaʔm	*Just/only women.*

164

(50) Pitjantjatjara (1/1)

50.1. If the Pitjantjatjara word derived from English has two syllables, then the first syllable of the borrowed word must have a long vowel.

50.2. NO. Words borrowed from English ones ending in a vowel sound or a non-rhotic "r", e.g., *teacher, paper, flour, crowbar*, keep that vowel which is written as 'a' in Pitjantjatjara. If the English word ends in a consonant (e.g., *bus, school*…), then the vowel 'a' is added to the Pitjantjatjara form.

50.3. **a.** p+l (**fl**our), s+k (**sch**ool), t+r (**dr**unk), k+r (**cr**owbar), w+p (cro**wb**ar). (The trickier ones are **sk** and **wb**. Some might consider that 'shovel' has a v+l sequence which is broken up in Pitj as *pil*.)

    b. *palawa, kuula, tarangka, kurupa* OR *flour, school, drunk, crowbar*.

    c. To avoid the sequences pl, tr and kr a vowel identical to the following vowel is placed between the consonant sounds; to avoid the sequences s+k (from *school*) or w+b (from *crowbar*) the first consonant is 'dropped'.

50.4. **a.** f, p, b, v (you might write bb, given 'rabbit' is one of the words).

    b. They are all pronounced by moving the bottom lip/jaw into contact with another part of the mouth (upper lip [p, b] or upper teeth [f,v], in order to stop or constrict the outgoing airflow).

50.5. **a.** Palata

    b. **1.** 'b' would be written as 'p'.
    2. The vowel sound written 'oo' in English would be written as 'a'.
    3. p+l sequence would be broken up by insertion of vowel 'a', as the English vowel sound in *blood* is written as 'a' (inserted vowel is a copy of the following vowel).
    4. The 'd' sound would be written as 't'.
    5. The word must end in 'a', so that vowel would be added./ OR English word ends in a consonant so 'a' must be added in Pitjantjatjara.

The Pitjantjatjara borrowed these words from speakers with a nonrhotic dialect (that is, who don't pronounce the final "r" in words like "car").

(51) String Transformers (1/1)

51.1. Strings 2, 3, 5, 7, 8, 10, and 11 can be generated. The template is $ax + bx + cy + bcd + dy$ (that is, x repetitions of the character 'a', followed by x repetitions of the character 'b', and so on).

51.2. There are a couple of possibilities. One option would be to add the rule $S \rightarrow B$. Another possibility would be allowing an empty right-side: $A \rightarrow \emptyset$, where $\emptyset$ means an empty string.

(52) Nen (1/1)

52.1. The translations are shown in the table.

a.	you (one person) talk	bám nowabte
b.	he (or she) returns	bè nánan̄gte
c.	they (three or more) return	bè nánan̄gtat
d.	we (three or more) talk	yánd nowabtam
e.	you two work	bám nogiabát

52.2. **a.** 'I' = *yánd*, plus the suffix/ending *t* on the root, plus the suffix *-an*.
b. 'they (more than two)' = *bè*, plus the suffix *t* on the root, plus the suffix *-at*.

52.3. **a.** *yánd* = 'Any set containing speaker // first person'.
b. *bè* = 'Any set not containing speaker or hearer // third person'.

52.4. One, or three or more—i.e., any number but two // any number less or greater than two. 'Non-dual' would be the most elegant term.

52.5. By omitting the *-t-* (after the stem/before the subject suffix, etc.) // by using the bare stem. The accented 'a' only occurs with the dual.

52.6. *bè neretat*

(53) Enga (1/1)

53.1.

Sentence	English	Enga
1 & 5	I	-o
2 & 6	you	-no
3,4, 7, 8, 9	he	-ámo

53.2.

Sentence	English	Enga
1 & 4	you	d-
2 & 3	me	d-
5-9	him	ma-

53.3. The forms in the different tenses:

7. mail̲iámo   8. maip̲iámo   9. mait̲ámo
   present   past   future

53.4. 1. dílio   2. dil̲ino   5. mail̲íno   9. mait̲ámo   [First 'i' should be circled]

53.5. Yes. The accent is always on the second to last (penultimate) syllable.

i. Given that **dílio** is pronounced as *dilyo* with two syllables, the accent is on the second to last syllable, which is the first syllable (i.e. on the first -i-).

ii. In **dilíno** and **diliámo**, the accent is on the second to last syllable.

iii. Given that **maílio** is pronounced as a three syllable word, *ma-i-lyo*, the accent falls on first -i-, as is the vowel in the second to last syllable.

53.6. When the agent ending *-me* is added to the pronoun, if the pronoun without this ending is accented on the first vowel (as seen when it is the second word of the sentence), then the accent stays on that vowel, otherwise it moves to the final syllable of the augmented word (OR to the ending/suffix *-me*), e.g., *émba + me > émba-me*; *baá + me > baa-mé*; *nambá + me > namba-mé*.

(54) News Tag (1/1)

The information retrieval engine incorrectly *stems* the words. The purpose of stemming is to merge related words such as "stable", "stabilize", "unstable", etc. by ignoring some prefixes and suffixes. In the sentences shown here, the specific mistakes are:

- retire → tire   (In the general case, this rule works: repaint → paint)
- dentist → dent   (artist → art)
- injury → jury   (insane → sane)
- ratify → rat   (beautify → beauty)
- irony → iron   (sugary → sugar)
- fluids → flu   (vapid → vapor)
- predated → predator (requested → requestor)

More examples:

number → numb (bolder → bold)
restore → store (rewrite → write)

(55) Hebrew (1/3)

Observations:

We see that sentences 1, 2 both have "shelo" and "his", and sentence 8 has "sheli" and "my", so "shelo" = "his" and "sheli" = "my". Since in sentence 2 "shelo" is sentence-final, the word order is "X + sheli/shelo" = "my/his X".

We find one "ha-" for every "the" in English:
1 – hamazleg – *the fork*
3 – hatarnególet – *the chicken*
7 – ha'isha, hayalda – *the woman, the girl*
9 – mehakinus – *the conference* (we know from question 3 that "me-" is another prefix, so mehakinus = me-ha-kinus)
10 – hashi'urim – *the homework*
11 – haxamor – *the donkey*
12 – hanasi – *the president*

We also find "ha-" in possesives:
1 – mehayad shelo – his hand (= me-ha-yad shelo)
2 – hasakin shelo – his knife
8 – hazahav sheli – my gold
The Hebrew expressions more literally are like the English "the hand of his", "the knife of his", "the gold of mine". Thus "ha-" = "the" (definite article).

Sentence 1 has "mehayad" and "from his hand", and sentence 9 has "mehakinus" and "from the conference", so the prefix "me-" means "from" and comes before "ha-".

We notice that some sentences have similar-looking words in English and in Hebrew which seem to correspond to each other:

| 1: kshera'a – *saw*
2: ra'íti – *saw*
6: ra'a – *saw*
7: ro'a – *sees* | 2: shoxet – *slaughterer*
3: eshxat – *slaughtered*
5: shoxatim – *slaughters* | 7: verokédet – *dancing*
8: rikud – *dance*
8: verakádeti – *danced* | 4: ekne – *buy*
8: kaníti – *bought* |

We see that in Hebrew related words share a root made up of consonants:

r-' = *sight*	sh-x-t = *slaughter*	r-k-d = *dance*	k-n = *buying*

Knowing that "rikud" = "dancing (noun)", we see that in sentence 8, "kaníti séfer al rikud" = "bought a book on dancing", so in Hebrew, the object comes after the verb. In sentence 1, we also know that "hamazleg" = "the fork" (since "ha-" = "the" and, per above, "mehayad shelo" = "from his hand"), so the subject comes before the verb, showing that Hebrew is an SVO (subject-verb-object) language. (In fact, more literary Hebrew tends to be VSO, but this is not relevant to the problem.)

170

(55) Hebrew (2/3)

The Hebrew word "et" (sentences 2, 7, 8, 10, 11, 12) is used before the (direct) object of a verb when the object is a definite noun (i.e., has the prefix "ha-"); we see that "et" is not used in sentences 1, 2, 4, 5, 6, 8 where the object is indefinite or a pronoun. (Thus in 2: "ra'íti shoxet" = "I saw a slaughterer", but "mexaded et hasakin shelo" = "sharpening his knife")

Pronominal objects: "oti" = "me" (sentence 1), "oto" = "it" (sentence 4).

We see that the prefix "ve-" corresponds to English "and" (7: verokédet = "and dancing"; 8: "verakádeti" = "and [I] danced"). Similarly in sentences 1 and 9 the conjunction "when" = Hebrew "kshe-".

In sentence 8, we have "maxárti et kol hazahav sheli"= "I sold all my gold", so since "et" introduces the direct object, "kol hazahav sheli" = "all my gold", "maxárti" = "I sold". Similarly, from sentence 11 "emkor" = "I will sell". Thus, verbs inflect for tense and subject person.

We can now arrange all the verb forms we have seen so far in a table ordered by tense and subject person. Verbs from question 3 are listed in parentheses, and their columns have been chosen by making a rough comparison of their appearance to that of the other verbs:

		PAST		PRESENT			FUTURE	
		I	he	he	she	they	I	you
1	k-n = buy	kaníti	(kana)	?	?	?	ekne	?
2	r-' = see	ra'íti	ra'a	?	ro'a	?	?	(tir'e)
3	n-f-l = fall	?	nafal	(nofel)	?	?	?	?
4	sh-x-t = slaughter	shaxáteti	?	shoxet	?	shoxatim	?	?
5	r-k-d = dance	rakádeti	?	?	rokédet	(rokdim)	?	?
6	x-z-r = return	?	xazar	?	?	?	?	?
7	m-k/x-r = sell	maxárti	?	?	?	moxrim	emkor	timkor
8	z-k/x-r = remember	?	?	?	?	zoxrim	?	?
9	s-x-k = play	sixákti	?	?	mesaxéket	(mesaxakim)	?	?
10	x-d-d = sharpen	(xidádeti)	?	mexaded	?	?	?	?
11	b-x-r = elect	?	?	?	?	boxarim	?	?

We place the verb "shoxatim" from sentence 5 in the "present-they" column because all other verbs that end in "-im" go in this column. This is how Hebrew marks generics ("one" does something).

We can summarize the conjugation patterns as follows. Each C represents a consonant. Verbs inflect by putting their root consonants in one of the following templates:

(55) Hebrew (3/3)

	PAST		PRESENT			FUTURE	
	I	he	he	she	they	I	you
C-C	CaCíti	CaCa	?	CoCa	?	eCCe	tiCCe
C-C-C (1)	CaCáC(e)ti	CaCaC	CoCeC	CoCéCet	CoC(a)Cim	eCCoC	tiCCoC
C-C-C (2)	CiCáC(e)ti	?	meCaCeC	meCaCéCet	meCaC(a)Cim	?	?

C-C is the groups of verbs with two root consonants, and C-C-C (1) and (2) are the two groups of verbs with three consonants.

We see that the optional vowel (e) is added after the consonants "t" and "d". We can explain this by using the logic of question 2. Older Hebrew had the consonant clusters "tt" and "dt", which now are no longer clusters because the vowel "e" has been inserted in them.

We see that in verb 7, the middle consonant alternates between "k" (emkor) and "x" (moxrim). Looking at assignment 1, we can guess that the "x" in "moxrim" was originally a "k" in older Hebrew. This allows us to solve question 1.

We see the optional vowel (a) is inserted in some verbs after "x", but not others. We suppose that this is another vowel inserted to break up older Hebrew consonant clusters. We see "a" inserted in "boxarim" but not "moxrim", so knowing that the "x" in "moxrim" was originally "k", we see that the consonant cluster "xr" had "a" inserted at a stage before "k" became "x". Similarly, in "mesaxakim" and "shoxatim", the original clusters were "xk" and "xt". This allows us to solve question 2.

From the above, we see that the "x" in "zoxrim" must have originally been "k", since "a" was not inserted into the cluster "kr", which became "xr". Thus "zoxrim" would also be an acceptable answer for question 2. This also shows that "I will remember" = "ezkor" rather than "ezxor", which is necessary for question 4.

Now that we know how to conjugate verbs and basic Hebrew word order, we can compare the example sentences to get enough basic vocabulary to solve questions 3 and 4.

55.1. moxrim, zoxrim (reasoning: see above)

55.2. tt; dt; xt; xr; xk (reasoning: see above)

55.3. **A.** You will see people playing and dancing outside.
B. The knife always falls on his hand.
C. I sharpened it and the slaughterer bought it.

55.4. **A.** Ezkor la'asot et hashi'urim sheli.
B. Lo tikne zahav bezol.
C. Ha'isha shoxétet et haxamor baxuc.

172

(56) Japanese Kanazukai (1/1)

56.1.

Kyuukanazukai	Shinkanazukai	English
Keushitsu	*Kyoushitsu*	Classroom
Wotoko	*Otoko*	Male
Tefu	*Chou*	Butterfly
Ikau	*Ikou*	Let's go
Kefu	*Kyou*	Today
Kifudai	*Kyuudai*	To pass an exam
Ahare	*Aware*	Sorrow

56.2. W, H, F disappear.
Exception: HA, WA → WA (disappearence of W, H only ordered by analogy with F)
1) EU → YOU; IU → YUU; AU → OU (this last shift might alternatively be placed after step 3)
2) SY → SH; TY → CH; JY → J

1 comes before 2, as seen in examples like jifuji → *jiuji → *jyuuji → juuji. 2 comes before 3, as seen in examples like deseu → *desyou → deshou. (* marks an unattested intermediate stage.)

Index of Languages (1/2)

D. Radev (ed.), *Puzzles in Logic, Languages and Computation: The Red Book*, Recreational Linguistics 1,
DOI 10.1007/978-3-642-34378-0, © Springer-Verlag Berlin Heidelberg 2013

Index of Languages (2/2)

Index of Computational Topics

D. Radev (ed.), *Puzzles in Logic, Languages and Computation: The Red Book*, Recreational Linguistics 1,
DOI 10.1007/978-3-642-34378-0, © Springer-Verlag Berlin Heidelberg 2013

Index of Other Topics

D. Radev (ed.), *Puzzles in Logic, Languages and Computation: The Red Book*, Recreational Linguistics 1,
DOI 10.1007/978-3-642-34378-0, © Springer-Verlag Berlin Heidelberg 2013

About the Editor

Dragomir Radev is the program chair of the North American Computational Linguistics Olympiad (NACLO). He has been the head coach of the US teams at the International Linguistics Olympiad (IOL) since 2007. He holds a PhD from Columbia University and is currently a Professor of Computer Science and Engineering, Information, and Linguistics at the University of Michigan and an Adjunct Professor of Computer Science at Columbia University. He also serves as the secretary of the Association for Computational Linguistics (ACL) and is an Association for Computing Machinery (ACM) Distinguished Scientist.

D. Radev (ed.), *Puzzles in Logic, Languages and Computation: The Red Book*, Recreational Linguistics 1,
DOI 10.1007/978-3-642-34378-0, © Springer-Verlag Berlin Heidelberg 2013

Printed by Publishers' Graphics LLC